THE
HORSE
FITNESS &
COMPETITION

withdrawn an

6

7

THE
HORSE
FITNESS &
COMPETITION

Julie Brega

J.A. Allen
London

British Library Cataloguing in Publication Data
A catalogue record for this book is available from the British Library

ISBN 0.85131.622.0

Published in Great Britain in 1996 by
J.A. Allen and Company Limited,
1 Lower Grosvenor Place,
Buckingham Palace Road,
London, SW1W 0EL.

Typeset in Hong Kong by Setrite Typesetters Ltd.
Printed in Hong Kong by Dah Hua Printing Press Co. Ltd.

CONTENTS

LIST OF
ILLUSTRATIONS

LIST OF TABLES

Table 5 is reproduced, with permission, from the article *The Vet Check* by Art King, published in *On to Atlanta '96* (ISBN 0-88955-380-7) by the Equine Research Centre, University of Guelph, Ontario, Canada NJG 2W1.

DEDICATION

I would like to dedicate this book to the memory of *The Tickler* — a very special competition horse who gave me so much good experience, and most importantly, confidence and fun.

ACKNOWLEDGEMENTS

I would like to thank the following friends for their invaluable help in the production of this book:

Debby Baker, for deciphering and typesetting the original manuscript.

Annalisa Barrelet, BVetMed, MS, Cert ESM, MRCVS, for veterinary editing and much expert advice.

Kitty Best, for the excellent illustrations.

Martin Diggle, for his patience and editing skills.

And special thanks to my family:
To my parents, John and Sheila Hollywood, who look after our children, Holly and Josh, so brilliantly, allowing me to get some work done, to my step-daughter, Zoe, for keeping the horses, office and myself organized, and finally to my husband, Bill, for his constant help and support.

INTRODUCTION

The Horse: Fitness and Competition is one of six books in the Progressive Series. This series forms the basis of an advanced open learning course offered by The Open College of Equestrian Studies.

The main objective of these books is to present the information needed by the equestrian enthusiast in a clear and logical manner. This information is invaluable to everyone interested in horses, whether in a professional capacity as a yard manager or examination trainee, or as a private horse-owner.

This book deals with the fittening and management of the horse in preparation for various competitions. The importance of regular exercise for all horses, whether competing or not, is discussed, as is the scale of work types and relative levels of fitness.

Since fittening work has a direct effect upon the respiratory and circulatory systems, and on the musculature, these topics are discussed in the context of the fittening process.

The techniques for getting horses fit both by the traditional method and by interval training are dealt with, including preparation, weekly work plans and ways of monitoring the levels of fitness achieved.

The section on stable management deals with topics such as stress in the competition horse, tack and equipment used for

xiii

work and in the different disciplines, and preparation for various forms of competition. The means of transporting horses and the regulations which apply to the vehicles are also dealt with, as is preparation of the horse for a long journey.

Consideration is then given to the care and management of horses competing in horse trials and the component disciplines, endurance rides, showing classes, point-to-points and polo. While emphasis is placed on maintaining health and soundness, the final chapter gives advice on how to deal with disorders which might arise in a competition environment.

1

THE NEED FOR FITNESS

There is a wide range of equestrian activities and competitions which may be enjoyed by horses and riders, of varying abilities and aspirations. However, whether taking part in a local long distance ride or competing in a three day event, attention must be paid to the most important aspect of preparation — the fitness programme.

The fitness level for any particular discipline is achieved through regular exercise over a period of time. It should be noted however, that all horses, whether competing or not, require exercise.

EXERCISE AND FITNESS

In the wild, horses spend their days roaming, exercising themselves freely, resting as and when they desire. Similarly, a grass-kept horse will exercise himself in the field — although this will not be sufficient to achieve and maintain fitness for competition and/or hunting.

It is important that a stabled horse is exercised and ideally turned out every day for the following reasons:

1) Exercise promotes the circulation of bodily fluids within the cardiovascular and lymphatic systems, thereby aiding their effective functioning. This circulation also promotes effective digestion and the removal of waste products (some waste products being excreted via the skin when the horse sweats).

2) The respiratory system is developed, so promoting an improved supply of oxygen to the muscles.

3) The muscles respond to the stimulation of schooling and exercise, becoming supple and well developed.

4) The horse will become mentally relaxed — horses who are under-exercised tend to be 'uptight' and difficult to handle.

There are occasions when it is not possible to exercise horses because of very bad weather, injury or illness. In the event of enforced rest the diet must be adapted as follows to avoid causing disorders of the digestive and circulatory systems:

Cut out high-energy foods completely; any concentrates should be in the form of non-heating cubes.

Increase the quantity of good quality meadow hay.

Occasionally feed a bran mash to give a slightly laxative effect.

Add limestone flour to boost calcium levels. (Bran has a low calcium: phosphorus ratio and its fibre component inhibits calcium uptake).

An exercised horse is not necessarily fit. To achieve fitness, the exercise and workload have to be increased gradually in a structured way.

The aim of fittening

The general aim of fittening a horse is to enable him to participate in a given discipline with minimum fatigue and risk of injury. He should be able to work for longer before fatigue occurs and compete without distress.

The requirements for each discipline will vary, for example an Advanced dressage horse must be supremely supple and very fit but, because of the different stresses placed on the various systems of the horse, he would not necessarily be fit to compete in, say, a point-to-point. The following list of work types is set out in an *approximate* ascending scale of fitness.

Work types and fitness levels

Light hacking and schooling.
Non-jumping showing classes.
Showing classes involving jumping (such as Working Hunter).
Riding club dressage competition.
Riding club showjumping competition.
Showjumping up to Foxhunter level.
Hunter trials.
Showjumping up to Grade A.
Riding club one day events.
32 km (20 mile) long distance rides.
BHS one day events — Novice.
Advanced dressage competition.
Hunting three times a fortnight.
BHS one day events — Intermediate to Advanced.
BHS two day events — Novice, Intermediate.
BHS/FEI three day events — Novice, Intermediate, Advanced.
Flat racing.
Point-to-pointing and National Hunt racing.

When assessing fitness it must be understood that different qualities are needed in varying degrees.
These qualities include:

Obedience.
Balance and rhythm.
Impulsion.
Suppleness.
Calmness.
Athleticism.
Jumping ability.
Speed.
Acceleration.
Stamina and endurance.

There are no real benefits in having a horse overfit, especially for the less demanding disciplines. If overfit, horses tend to take longer to settle down at a competition venue, can be difficult to handle and need more work to maintain calmness.

When fittening horses, the overriding factor to be considered is that of *individuality*. Every horse is different and, depending upon temperament, age, soundness and the type of competition chosen, the fitness programme must suit each individual horse. The nature and length of the programme will also be affected by the following:

Time of year. If a horse has been out on lush grass and is overweight, he will take longer to get fit than if he had rested over the winter, rugged up, partially stabled and corn fed.

Age. It is more difficult and potentially damaging to achieve full fitness of a very young horse, since youngsters are physically immature.

Temperament. The keen, lighter, Thoroughbred type will be easier to get fit than a lazy, heavier sort.

Soundness. Any problem associated with soundness will result in much more time being needed, particularly with the early slow work.

Level of training. A horse who has already been fully fit once before will be easier to get fit again.

Having embarked upon a fitness programme the trainer must always apply common sense. Through observation, the horse's mental attitude, condition and soundness can be monitored and any adjustments made as necessary. Further to this, the programme should not be rigid; whilst a routine is essential a little flexibility allows important adjustments to be made.

Stress is a necessary factor in the fitness programme. Without stress the body will not adapt and develop. The skill lies in knowing how much stress to exert − *distress* can lead to damage, both mental and physical. Therefore, the horse must be exposed to gradually increasing levels of stress and must be allowed rest periods for recovery to prevent overstressing. Such gradual introduction of stress enables the systems of the horse to adapt and alter, thereby preparing them for similar levels of stress in the future.

Eventually the horse will reach his peak of fitness — at this point the stress cannot be increased further without the risk of souring the horse or causing physical damage. Once peak fitness has been achieved, the objective is to maintain it for only as long as is necessary. For example, an eventer does not need to be at peak fitness for the whole season — his peak should be reached for the major event or events.

2

PHYSIOLOGICAL CONSIDERATIONS

When getting a horse fit, the efficiency of the respiratory and circulatory systems have to be developed in order to increase the horse's capacity to draw in oxygen, transport it to the muscles for use in energy production and remove the waste products of this process. Also, the muscles and tendons have to become durable and strong — increased use leads to an improved supply of nutrients and oxygen which, over a period of time, results in the development of increasingly stronger tissue.

Thus, in order to understand how horses become fit, it is necessary to have some knowledge of the relevant systems. These are covered in detail in two other books in the series: *The Horse: Physiology* and *The Horse: The Foot, Shoeing and Lameness*, but the following information summarizes those points most relevant to fitness and soundness.

THE RESPIRATORY SYSTEM

The functions of the respiratory system are:

Upon inhalation, to draw into the lungs air, which supplies oxygen, a gas essential for life.

Within the lungs, to transfer the oxygen from the air into the bloodstream.

To transfer carbon dioxide, the waste product of energy production, from the bloodstream to the lungs.

To expel carbon dioxide upon exhalation.

There are two types of respiration:

External respiration (breathing) is the transfer of gases between the external environment and the blood, and takes place within the airways of the head and neck and the lungs.

Cell, tissue or internal respiration is the metabolic breakdown of organic compounds, mainly carbohydrates, which occurs throughout the cells of the body, resulting in the release of energy.

   Oxygen is normally required for the chemical reactions necessary for maintaining life. These reactions are controlled by enzymes. Once the energy has been released, the end products are carbon dioxide and water. Oxygen is transferred from the blood to all cells and carbon dioxide is transferred from these cells to the blood.

Anatomy of the respiratory system

The respiratory system consists of the airways (upper respiratory tract) and the lungs (lower respiratory tract).

THE AIRWAYS
The nostrils. Air is drawn in through the nostrils; the horse is not able to breath in through his mouth.

The nasal cavities. These contain the turbinate bones which are covered with mucous membranes which warm and clean the incoming air. Tiny hairlike cilia project from these membranes and trap dust particles. The warmed air passes on to the pharynx.

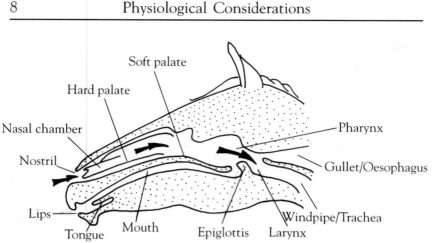

Figure 1 The anatomy of the upper respiratory tract

The pharynx. This chamber at the back of the throat is used by both the respiratory and digestive systems. A musculo-membranous partition, the soft palate, separates the two systems' entrances into this chamber. The epiglottis overlaps the soft palate. During the process of breathing, it allows air to pass through to the larynx. When the horse swallows food, the epiglottis covers the larynx and the soft palate moves up to allow the food to pass into the oesophagus without interfering with the breathing process.

The larynx. This complex mechanism is situated at the top of the trachea and consists of interconnected cartilages, muscle and fibrous tissues covered by mucous membrane. Among these fibrous tissues are the vocal cords which, when vibrated by the forced passage of air, create sounds. The function of the larynx, apart from that of producing the voice, is to ensure that only gases pass into the deeper regions of the respiratory system; the larynx closes as soon as food particles touch the pharynx.

The trachea. The trachea, or windpipe, extends from the larynx down to the lungs and is permanently held open by rings of cartilage. Close to the lungs, the trachea branches into the two bronchi. The trachea is lined by millions of hairlike cilia, which assist in removing mucus by their wavelike motion.

LOWER RESPIRATORY TRACT

The bronchi. These tubes are held open by thin rings of cartilage and each enter one lung, where they then continue to divide, forming a bronchial 'tree'. The branches get progressively smaller, the narrowest being known as bronchioles.

The bronchioles. These very narrow tubes are lined with a continuation of the ciliated mucous membrane and are not supported by cartilaginous rings. The smallest of the bronchioles are known as respiratory bronchioles, each of which then further divide into alveolar ducts.

The alveoli at the end of each duct are air sacs which make up the lung tissue. There are millions of thin-walled alveoli, giving a huge surface area — estimated at several hundred square metres. In order to keep the airways moist, a thin film of mucus is secreted by cells lining the alveoli. In a healthy horse the mucus never accumulates to a serious degree.

Permeating through the alveoli are the capillaries of the pulmonary artery. It is here that gaseous exchange occurs. The thin film of liquid secreted by the alveoli also acts as a medium for diffusion. The deoxygenated blood in the capillaries is very close to the surface of the alveoli. The carbon dioxide within this blood diffuses into the air in the alveoli and is expelled when the horse breathes out. Oxygen diffuses from the air into the alveoli, through the thin capillary walls, and combines with the haemoglobin in the blood.

External respiration

Inhalation occurs as a result of expansion of the rib cage, which causes the dome-shaped diaphragm (the muscular sheet dividing the chest from the abdomen) to contract and flatten, so enlarging the thorax and reducing the air pressure within the lungs to below that of the external environment. This difference in pressure causes air to be pulled into the respiratory system through the nostrils, thus increasing the pressure in the lungs

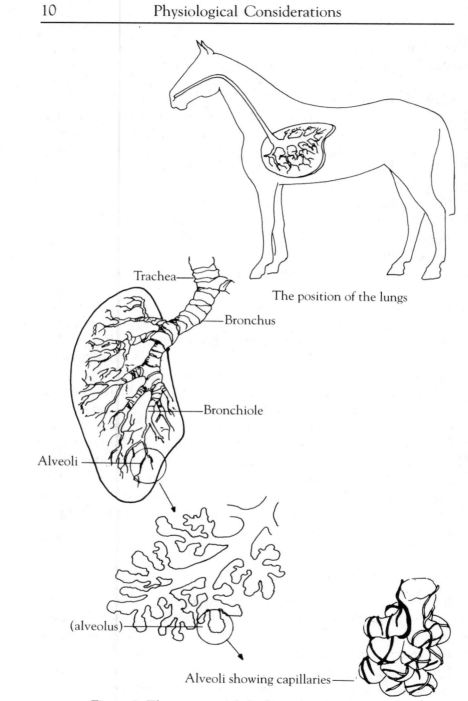

The position of the lungs

Trachea

Bronchus

Bronchiole

Alveoli

(alveolus)

Alveoli showing capillaries

Figure 2 The anatomy of the lower respiratory tract

to equal the external air pressure. As the ribs recoil to their original position, so the diaphragm relaxes and returns to its dome-shaped position.

Exhalation occurs as the chest volume decreases and the pressure within the thoracic cavity increases, forcing air out of the lungs. Exhalation is mainly a passive process but the trunk muscles can assist by pushing the gut contents against the diaphragm. The diaphragm begins just in front of the loins and slopes downwards and forwards to the breastbone.

Internal (tissue) respiration

Internal respiration occurs when the oxygen in the blood (oxyhaemoglobin) reaches the body tissue. A series of chemical reactions causes energy to be produced from glucose in the blood or glycogen in muscle cells. This energy is stored in energy molecules and can be released as needed. This process is known as aerobic respiration, the end product of which is carbon dioxide. This waste product attaches to the haemoglobin in the blood and is carried to the lungs, from where it is expelled.

During heavy and strenuous exercise, the demands of the body may not be supplied by the oxygen arriving in the blood. In this case, respiration takes place anaerobically, that is, without oxygen. The end product of anaerobic respiration is lactic acid. Lactic acid is removed in the bloodstream and transported to the liver for detoxification. If the acid is allowed to build up in the muscle cells, it will give rise to fatigue and possibly cramp-like feelings, such as muscle fatigue and/or tying-up syndrome.

Anaerobic respiration does not produce so much energy as aerobic respiration and, since the end product is poisonous, it is desirable to avoid working a horse strenuously beyond his level of fitness for any length of time. Oxygen is essential for the removal of lactic acid so, after strenuous work, the horse will 'blow' for much longer as his lungs strive to draw in air and pay off the 'oxygen debt' which has arisen as a result of prolonged anaerobic respiration.

The release of energy during the process of internal respiration, and the problems associated with anaerobic respiration are dealt with in further detail in two other books in the series — *The Horse: General Management* and *The Horse: Physiology*. The determination of the anaerobic threshold, as an assessment of fitness, is described further on in this book (Monitoring to Assess Fitness).

The effect of work upon the respiratory system

The normal rate of breaths per minute in the adult horse at rest is between 8 and 16. Youngstock have a slightly higher rate. During strenuous exercise the rate may increase to 120 breaths per minute in order to cope with the body's extra oxygen requirements. At canter and gallop, the respiratory rate is locked to the stride rate.

One aim of fitness work is to increase a horse's ability to supply and utilize oxygen. The unfit horse does not have so great a functional lung capacity as a fit one because not all of the alveoli (air sacs) are recruited. Upon exercise of an unfit horse there may be a slight nasal discharge. This may result from a sub-clinical infection, which may also cause an enlargement of the lymph follicles in the lining of the throat (lymphoid hyperplasia, or 'thick in the wind').

As fitness progresses so more alveoli become clear, thus increasing the functional capacity of the lungs. This is known as alveolar recruitment. As the surface area of useful lung tissue increases, so the capillaries surrounding the alveoli proliferate. This pulmonary capillarization provides a greater surface area for the increased gaseous exchange necessary in the working horse.

As the horse's workload increases, so his muscles will develop. This will include the muscles of the diaphragm and chest, further aiding efficient breathing.

THE CIRCULATORY SYSTEM

The circulatory system consists of a network of vessels carrying blood pumped by the heart to every part of the body. The circulating blood transports essential substances:

Oxygen from the lungs to all of the body cells.

Carbon dioxide from body cells to the lungs.

Nutrients and *water* from the gut or storage organs (fat) to the body cells.

Hormones from the endocrine glands to the body cells.

Antibodies (defence force) from the lymphatic system to sites of injury or infection.

Heat from the centre of the body or working muscles, distributed or dissipated as required.

Waste products from the body cells to the liver and/or kidneys for detoxification/excretion.

Sixty per cent of an adult horse's bodyweight (including blood) is water. Blood plays a vital role in regulating the balance of fluids within the body, which is particularly important in the case of a horse sweating heavily. As blood circulates, it gains and loses substances as follows:

Site	Gains	Loses
Lungs	Oxygen	Carbon dioxide
Intestines	Dissolved nutrients	Oxygen
Body tissues	Carbon dioxide, lactic acid	Oxygen
Liver	Urea	Glucose (stored as glycogen)
Endocrine glands	Hormones	Oxygen
Kidneys	Hormones (renin and erythropoietin)	Salts, water, urea

The composition of blood

Blood is a complex vital substance, the main components of which are plasma, red and white cells and platelets.

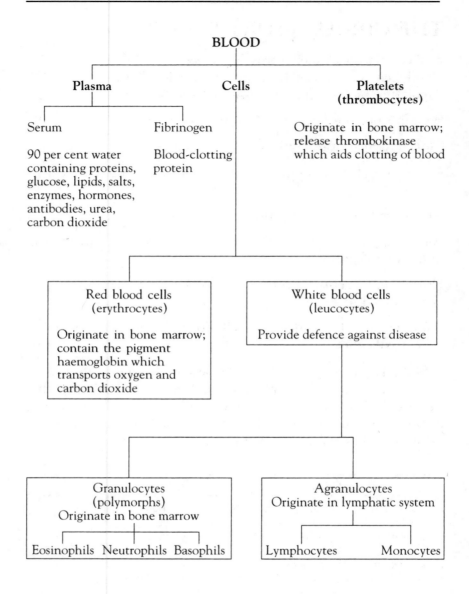

Figure 3 The composition of blood

Plasma

Plasma is a straw coloured liquid composed of serum and fibrinogen, in which all of the other components of blood are suspended.

Serum is 90 per cent water and contains dissolved organic substances: amino acids, lipids, glucose, salts and minerals, blood proteins (including antibodies), urea, hormones, enzymes and carbon dioxide.

Fibrinogen is the important blood clotting protein.

   In blood samples, plasma is the fluid which can be collected from a sample which has been prevented from clotting.

Red blood cells

The main function of the red blood corpuscles (erythrocytes) is to carry oxygen from the lungs to the tissues. They are in the shape of biconcave discs which have no nucleus. They are constantly being worn out and replaced. Worn cells are destroyed in the spleen and liver and by-products are excreted in the bile. New cells are produced in the bone marrow. This process of renewal is speeded up as the horse works harder and faster. Red blood corpuscles contain haemoglobin, the pigment which can bind with oxygen and carbon dioxide. Oxygen is carried from the lungs to the bodily tissues as oxyhaemoglobin. Upon reaching needy tissues the oxygen detaches from the haemoglobin and is diffused through the fine capillary walls. Some carbon dioxide is carried away from the tissue as carboxyhaemoglobin; the rest is dissolved in plasma.

White blood cells

The white blood cells, leucocytes, are colourless and almost transparent. They are larger than red cells but approximately a thousand times less numerous. Their chief function is to defend the body against disease. They can squeeze through the blood vessel walls to accumulate at sites of injury or infection.

There are five types of white blood cells. The first category, known as granulocytes or polymorphs, originate in the red bone marrow and are divided into:

Neutrophils (approx. 60 per cent) which are a defence against acute infection. They engulf invading pathogens, which are then digested by enzymes. Once a neutrophil is full it dies, resulting in the production of pus.

Basophils (less than 2 per cent) which control inflammation by releasing histamine.

Eosinophils (less than 3 per cent) which detoxify foreign proteins by producing enzymes which help break them down.

The second category of white blood cells, known as agranulocytes, originate in the lymphatic system and consist of:

Lymphocytes (approx. 40 per cent) which produce antibodies specific to invading pathogens in order to render them harmless.

Monocytes (less than 2 per cent) which are concerned with less acute infection.

Platelets

These are the smallest of the blood cells. They originate in the red bone marrow. Platelets release thrombokinase which helps with the process of blood clotting.

Blood vessels

These are the structures through which blood travels to circulate the body. There are three types of blood vessel: arteries, veins and capillaries. Arteries and veins are mostly named according to the organ that they serve, examples being pulmonary (lungs), renal (kidneys), hepatic (liver) and mesenteric (gut).

The characteristics of the main blood vessels can be summarized thus:

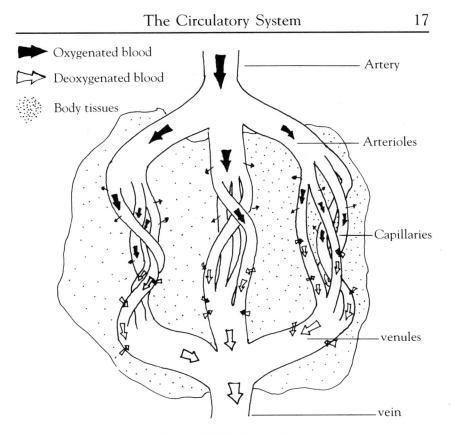

Figure 4 Blood vessels

Arteries

Carry blood away from the heart.

Carry oxygenated blood (except pulmonary artery).

Blood is carried at high pressure.

Narrow bore, highly elastic, to maintain pressure. Widen with heartbeat, giving a pulse.

Thick, muscular walls.

No valves.

Branch into arterioles.

Veins

Carry blood to the heart.

Carry deoxygenated blood (except pulmonary vein).

Blood is carried at low pressure.

Wide bore.

Thin walls.

Valves to prevent backflow.

Collect from venules.

The capillaries are a network of threadlike vessels extending from arterioles and venules, reaching into every part of the body. Capillaries carrying oxygenated arterial blood converge with those which carry away deoxygenated venous blood. The thin walls of capillaries, one cell in thickness, allow the diffusion of oxygen and dissolved nutrients into the tissues and the removal of carbon dioxide and waste matter. From the capillaries, polymorphs escape to sites of injury to fight infection. The very narrow bore slows the flow of blood between the arteries and veins.

The heart

The heart is situated in the thoracic cavity between the lungs. It is a hollow, muscular organ which can be considered as two pumps working simultaneously. The heart is composed of specialized cardiac muscle which does not fatigue. The average horse of 500 kg (1100 1b) has a heart weighing approximately 4 kg (9 lb).

The heart consists of four chambers; two upper chambers known as atria and two lower chambers known as ventricles. The atria receive blood from the large veins, the ventricles pump the blood out through the large arteries.

The heartbeat

The heartbeat works as follows. Blood enters the left and right atria at the same time. Once full, the atria contract and the valves dividing the atria and ventricles open as the blood is pushed through into the relaxed ventricles. When the ventricles are nearly full they contract, causing the valves to slam shut, pushing the blood out through the arteries. One-way valves prevent a backflow of blood. The action of heart muscle relaxing before and during the process of filling is known as the diastolic action. The contraction of the heart muscle as it empties is known as the systolic action.

The sound heard when listening to the heartbeat is a very distinct 'lubb-dup'. This can be heard between 36 and 42 times per minute in a healthy adult horse at rest. The 'lubb' sound occurs as the valves between the atria and ventricles close and as the arterial exit valves open, so allowing the blood out to the lungs and body. The harder sounding 'dup' denotes the opening of the valves between the heart chambers and the closing of the arterial valves. The period of silence denotes the heart filling with blood.

The circulation of blood

The heartbeat (assisted, to some extent, by the action of various muscles within the body) powers the two systems of circulation which make up the double circulation of blood within the horse. These are the pulmonary circulation of blood through the lungs and the systemic circulation of blood through the body.

Pulmonary circulation

Deoxygenated blood arrives via the vena cava in the right atrium and then moves down through the tricuspid valve to the right ventricle from where it is pumped through the pulmonary artery into the capillary network of the lungs. Here, carbon dioxide is released through the capillary walls into the alveoli, from which it is expelled during the process of expiration. Diffusion of oxygen across the thin membranes of the alveoli also reoxygenates the blood, which then travels back through the pulmonary vein to the left atrium.

Systemic circulation

Reoxygenated blood moves down through the bicuspid valve from the left atrium to the left ventricle, from where it is pumped out under great pressure through the aorta to the body. Because of the need to send the oxygenated blood out at high pressure, the muscular wall of the left ventricle is thicker and stronger than that of the right ventricle.

The first branches are the coronary arteries which supply the heart muscle itself. The many other branches supply every organ of the body, with the first major branch, known as the

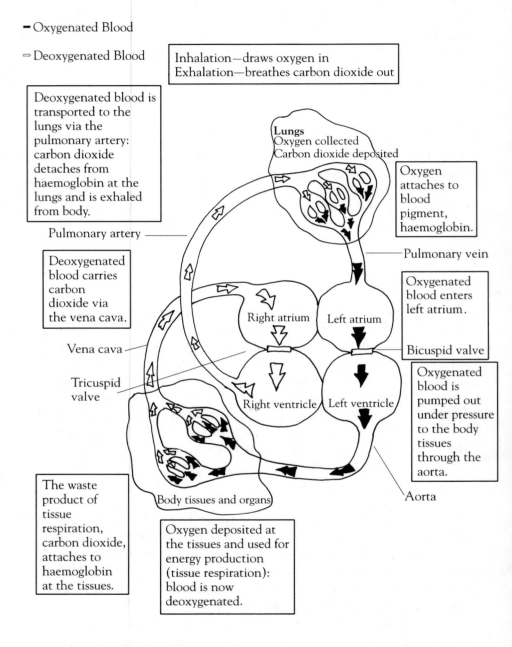

→ Oxygenated Blood

⇒ Deoxygenated Blood

Inhalation—draws oxygen in
Exhalation—breathes carbon dioxide out

Deoxygenated blood is transported to the lungs via the pulmonary artery: carbon dioxide detaches from haemoglobin at the lungs and is exhaled from body.

Lungs
Oxygen collected
Carbon dioxide deposited

Oxygen attaches to blood pigment, haemoglobin.

Pulmonary artery

Pulmonary vein

Deoxygenated blood carries carbon dioxide via the vena cava.

Right atrium

Left atrium

Oxygenated blood enters left atrium.

Vena cava

Bicuspid valve

Tricuspid valve

Right ventricle

Left ventricle

Oxygenated blood is pumped out under pressure to the body tissues through the aorta.

Aorta

Body tissues and organs

The waste product of tissue respiration, carbon dioxide, attaches to haemoglobin at the tissues.

Oxygen deposited at the tissues and used for energy production (tissue respiration): blood is now deoxygenated.

Figure 5 Basic pulmonary and systemic circulation

brachiocephalic, supplying the head and forelegs. The aorta then passes through the diaphragm where a large branch off, the coeliac artery, supplies the stomach, liver and spleen. The mesenteric arteries supply the intestines — the large cranial at the front and the smaller caudal to the rear.

The blood from the intestines is collected in the hepatic portal vein which then subdivides into a capillary network within the liver. The blood is filtered in the liver before going back into general circulation via the hepatic vein which joins the vena cava.

The kidneys are supplied by the renal artery, while the hindquarters are supplied by the iliac arteries. The veins carrying the deoxygenated blood away from the organs and their tissues all converge with the vena cava to enter the heart at the right atrium.

Fitness and the circulatory system

Training and fitness work have a very noticeable effect upon the circulatory system. As the duration and level of exercise increase the muscles contract more often, resulting in the need for more oxygen and the removal of more waste products.

In order to cope with these extra demands the circulatory system has to work efficiently. With work, the heart becomes increasingly efficient: the amount of blood pumped with each heartbeat (the cardiac output) increases. The heart also increases in size.

As a response to the increase in demand for oxyen and removal of waste products, more capillares are formed, so giving a greater surface area for the process of gaseous exchange. In an unfit horse these adaptations are reversed. A fit horse will:

1) As a result of increased cardiac output have a slower resting heart rate (may be as low as 26 beats per minute).

2) Show a less marked increase in heart and respiratory rates after strenuous exercise.

3) Recover after exercise more quickly, that is, the respiratory and heart rates return to normal more quickly. (When the horse gallops, his heart rate may reach a maximum of 260 beats per minute).

During strenuous exercise, especially in an unfit horse, it is difficult for the body to provide enough oxygen for the muscle cells to cope with the workload. The muscles are forced to work anaerobically, resulting in lactic acid production. When lactic acid accumulates in the muscles, muscular fatigue and pain result. The oxygen debt is 'paid off' after the exercise and it is this which causes the respiratory rate to continue to be elevated when the horse is 'cooling-off'.

MUSCLES, TENDONS AND LIGAMENTS

Movement is initiated through the combined effect of the activities of skeletal muscle, tendons and ligaments upon the skeleton. Each is a different form of connective tissue with its own distinct function. By contracting, muscles cause movement of bones. The muscles are attached to these bones by tendons. Ligaments connect many of the bones and cartilages to each other.

Muscles

Muscles are divided into three main types:

Smooth muscles are involuntary muscles (not under conscious control) found in the digestive and reproductive tracts, the blood vascular system, bladder and bowels.

Cardiac muscles are specialized muscles found only in the heart.

Skeletal or striated muscles are attached to, support and move the skeleton. It is the skeletal muscles which form the 'meat' of the horse and are responsible for locomotion. It is with these that we are chiefly concerned here.

Skeletal muscles are under the voluntary control of the horse and amount to approximately one third of the bodyweight, there being, on average, seven hundred skeletal muscles in the body. The functions of these muscles are:

1) To support the skeletal structure.

2) To move the skeleton through contraction of the muscle fibres.

3) To maintain joint stability, preventing undesirable, excessive movement.

4) Heat production by shivering.

Muscles contract to bring about an action: flexor muscles contract causing the joint to flex. The joint is then straightened by contraction of the corresponding extensor muscle. (Extension of a muscle is always a passive process, each muscle group being opposed by another with an antagonistic effect.) Abductor muscles carry the limb away from the mid-line of the body whilst adductor muscles carry the limb towards it.

In order for muscles to perform these functions they have attachments at either end: the origin, which tends to be the less movable part and the insertion, the more movable part. Upon contraction the insertion generally moves towards the origin. The attachments may be directly onto the skeleton, or via a connection of deep fascia (fibrous tissue).

Composition of skeletal muscle

Muscle bellies (the typical muscle forms) come in various shapes and sizes. Some are flat and sheet-like, for example the latissimus dorsi, external abdominal oblique and trapezius. In these the muscle fibres are long, with flattened tendinous attachments, offering a wide range of movement.

Long, strap-like muscles such as the brachiocephalic also have long fibres, but the muscles of the forearm and thigh have shorter fibres densely packed in the belly, resulting in great strength. Such muscles are known as pennate muscles.

All skeletal muscle is composed of millions of long, slender fibres known as myofibrils. Each fibre is a single cell, elongated and cylindrical. These fibres lie parallel to each other, supported and bound by connective tissue within the muscle belly. This connective tissue binds the muscle fibres to the tendons at either end. When stimulated by a nervous impulse, the myofibrils slide over one another with a ratchet-type mechanism, causing the muscle to shorten, thicken and therefore contract — the muscle fibres themselves do not actually shorten.

Muscle contraction

The contraction of muscles requires a supply of energy. In addition to the myofibrils, muscle contains tiny intracellular organs called mitochondria. These store the carbohydrate energy-giving substance glycogen, which is broken down to release energy through a chemical reaction caused by enzymes, which are also stored within the muscle cells. To fuel this process, oxygen is brought to the muscles by the blood supply and is stored in the red muscle pigment, myoglobin. Myoglobin is a protein which can bind oxygen to itself.

As a result of muscular activity, waste products such as carbon dioxide are produced. These waste products are removed via the bloodstream as previously described.

Determining muscle fibre types

The fibres that make up muscle vary in speed of contraction and ability to utilize oxygen. Although the basic muscle fibre type is determined by genetics, with training some of the muscle fibre qualities may be enhanced.

Muscle fibres are referred to as slow-twitch or fast-twitch.

Slow-twitch fibres contract slowly and are known as Type I fibres. A horse with a high proportion of Type I fibres will be suited to endurance work rather than sprint type work. All slow-twitch fibres are high oxidative that is, they are particularly efficient at breaking down glycogen (glycolytic) and utilizing oxygen; they have a high aerobic capacity. Such fibres are narrow, and well supplied with capillaries. They tend to be flat rather than bulky — hence successful endurance horses tend to be light, without conspicuous muscular development.

Fast-twitch fibres. These are referred to a *Type II fibres* and are further divided into categories A and B.

Type IIA fibres are fast-contracting, high oxidative/glycolytic fibres which are versatile enough to provide power for both speed and endurance. They are responsive to conditioning and can be used for both aerobic and anaerobic respiration. Muscles trained for power tend to be bulky as the cross-sectional area of the fibres determines the force generated when the fibres contract.

Type IIB fibres are fast-contracting, low oxidative fibres ideal for a sprinter. A horse with a high proportion of Type IIB fibres would tire fairly quickly after a short burst at maximum speed.

Thus there are three distinct muscle fibre types:

Type I — Slow-twitch high oxidative (endurance).

Type IIA — Fast-twitch high oxidative/glycolytic (speed and endurance).

Type IIB — Fast-twitch glycolytic (sprint).

All horses have a mixture of the three types, the proportions of which are genetically determined. A knowledge of a horse's muscle fibre type helps to assess his potential for the various sports as well as giving a guide as to the physical state of the muscle — whether or not it is fittened.

The muscle fibre types may be identified and examined by means of a muscle biopsy. A local anaesthetic is given and a small incision made in the skin. Generally, the middle gluteal muscle in the hindquarters is used as it plays a very important role in propelling the horse forwards. A 3—5 mm biopsy needle is inserted into the muscle through the incision and 100—200 mg of muscle tissue is withdrawn and immediately frozen.

At the laboratory, the tissue is sectioned and various chemical stains used to aid the evaluation of the sample under an electron microscope. The biopsy can show the following:

1) Proportion of the various fibre types.

2) Size of each fibre type.

3) Aerobic potential of each fibre.

4) The amount of fuel — glycogen, fat, etc. stored in each fibre.

During training, the oxidative capacity of a fibre increases and likewise, during periods of inactivity, it decreases.

Tendons

A tendon is a fibrous cord of connective tissue continuous with the fibres of a muscle, attaching the muscle to bone, cartilage or other muscle. Tendons insert into bone or cartilage by means of small spikules known as 'Sharpey's fibres'. Where a muscle needs a wide area of attachment the tendon spreads out to form an aponeurosis. Where a tendon is in a position to rub against bone or other hard surfaces, it is enclosed in a sheath. This takes the form of an inner sheath which encloses and is firmly attached to the tendon, and an outer connective tissue

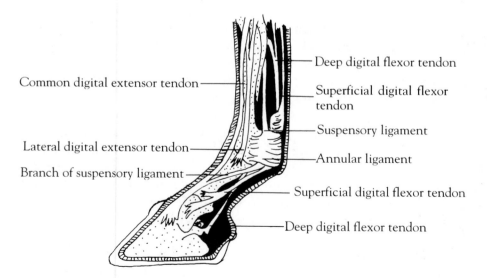

Common digital extensor tendon

Lateral digital extensor tendon

Branch of suspensory ligament

Deep digital flexor tendon

Superficial digital flexor tendon

Suspensory ligament

Annular ligament

Superficial digital flexor tendon

Deep digital flexor tendon

Figure 6 **The tendons and ligaments of the lower leg**

tube which is attached to its surrounding surface. The space between the two sheaths is filled with a lubricant similar to synovial fluid.

Tendons form in the embryo from fibroblasts (fibre-forming cells) which proliferate, becoming tightly packed, as the tendon grows. As development continues, the fibres become arranged in longitudinal rows and secrete collagen, the main supporting protein of connective tissue. The production of collagen is a continuous process — it takes six months to renew completely the collagen within a lower limb tendon. Excess, old or damaged collagen is broken down by enzymes and removed via the bloodstream. The blood supply through tendons is poor and, in the event of injury, it becomes disrupted, leading to reduced nutrient and oxygen supply which hampers the healing process.

The tendons of the lower leg

There are four tendons in the lower foreleg — two extensors on the front and two flexors on the back. They are:

The common digital extensor tendon (CDET). This tendon is attached to all of the bones in the foot except the navicular. It runs from the insertion of the CDE muscle, down the front of the cannon bone and over the fetlock joint towards the lower end of the long pastern bone. Here the tendon receives re-inforcement on either side from extensor branches of the suspensory ligament, which increases its width, enabling it to pass over the pastern joint, the short pastern bone, the pedal (coffin) joint and attach to the upper aspect of the pointed centre of the pedal bone (the pyramidal arch or extensor process). It is held in position by the bands from the suspensory ligament and by ligaments originating from the lower end of the long pastern bone.

The function of the CDET is to transfer the pull of the CDE muscle and extend the lower limb and foot.

The lateral digital extensor tendon (LDET). The LDE muscle lies behind the common digital extensor muscle. The tendons of these muscles run down in close contact with each other, the lateral digital extensor lying to the rear of the other and inserting into the outer side of the long pastern bone.

Working in conjunction with the CDE, the function of the LDE is to help straighten and extend the lower limb and foot.

The deep digital flexor tendon (DDFT). The muscle of this tendon originates at the ulna. The DDFT passes over the back of the knee through the carpal canal where it is held in position by the flexor retinaculum, a fascia sheet extending down from the flexor muscle. The DDFT is linked to the carpal bones by the carpal check ligament before extending down the back of the cannon bone between the superficial digital flexor tendon and the suspensory ligament. The carpal synovial sheath extends down-ward to enclose both the deep and superficial digital flexor tendons to the middle of the cannon bone. At this point, the DDFT is joined by its check ligament, the inferior (or carpal) check ligament. The digital synovial sheath surrounds the flexor tendons from a quarter of the way up the cannon bone to midway down the short pastern. The tendon then passes over the sesamoid bones, sliding on a glistening pad formed by the inter-sesamoidean ligament, before passing between the two extensions of the superficial digital flexor tendon. At this point the DDFT becomes broad and fanlike, passing over the navicular bone before inserting onto the lower surface of the pedal bone.

The superficial digital flexor tendon (SDFT). This tendon passes down the back of the cannon bone completely covering the DDFT. At the upper end of the pastern joint the SDFT divides into two branches, which insert on the upper and lower aspects of the short pastern.

The palmar annular ligament binds the SDFT, DDFT and their tendon sheath to the fetlock joint in the sesamoid groove. It blends with the SDFT and the collateral ligaments of the sesamoid bones.

The SDFT and DDFT extend down from their muscles in the forearm through to the foot, providing weight-bearing support and preventing the overextension of the fetlock joint (a role in which they are assisted by the check ligament). Their other chief function, when the horse is in motion, is to flex the joints of the lower leg.

The anatomy of the lower leg is discussed in greater depth in another book in this series, *The Horse: The Foot, Shoeing and Lameness*.

Ligaments

Ligaments are composed of bands of white and yellow fibrous tissue, the white being inelastic and the yellow, elastic. They are somewhat flexible but tough and unyielding in consistency. Ligaments can be categorized as follows:

Supporting or *suspending*, for example the suspensory ligament.

Annular — broad bands composed of deep fascia which direct the pull on a tendon.

Inter-osseus — tie bones together, for example the pedal and navicular.

Funicular or *cordlike* — hold bones together, for example between the cervical vertebrae.

Ligaments help to limit the movement of joints according to their functions, for example the fetlock, pastern and coffin joints have collateral ligaments on their inner and outer aspects to confine movement to forward and backward only. Ligaments attach to the bone through blending with the periosteum. They usually allow a certain amount of movement; the more that is required, the more yellow elastic tissue is present in that ligament. Conversely, those ligaments holding an immovable joint together will be composed only of inelastic white tissue.

Ligaments are poorly supplied with blood but rich in sensory nerves. Because of the poor blood supply they are very slow to heal after injury. Ligaments do not withstand prolonged stretching. If a joint is forced beyond the limitations set by the ligament, then a very painful sprain will occur. However, since ligaments (and muscles) are usually more elastic than the bone to which they are attached, any sudden, severe stress is more likely to break the bone than dislocate the joint or rupture the ligament.

Ligaments of the lower leg

The suspensory ligament. This lies between the two splint bones close to the back of the cannon bone, originating close to the knee and descending towards the fetlock joint, above which it divides into two branches. Each branch attaches to the corresponding sesamoid bone while some fibres pass to the front of the limb to blend in with the common digital extensor tendon. The suspensory ligament provides a form of support for the fetlock joint, preventing it from extending downward too far towards the ground, which would increase the risk of strains.

Check ligaments. The inferior check ligament, below the knee, acts to prevent undue strain being applied to the flexor tendons and to assist in supporting the horse, thus allowing him to sleep while standing. This ligament is connected to the deep flexor tendon. There is also a superior check ligament above the knee which connects to the superficial flexor tendon at the back of the humerus. This acts to assist the inferior check ligament.

3

THE FITTENING
PROCESS

When planning a fittening programme and calculating the time needed to achieve the required level of fitness, it is necessary to know the date of your first main event. For the purposes of example, we shall assume that this is to be a BHS Novice Horse Trial; as an approximate guide, once he has been brought up from grass, ten weeks should be sufficient time in which to produce a horse ready for this level of competition.

Before starting to get a horse fit, the following checks should be made:

Feet. The horse must be well shod, with stud holes if necessary.

Vaccinations. These must be given as protection against tetanus and equine influenza. Follow the vet's advice regarding time off after vaccination.

Worming. A worm burden will prevent the horse from utilizing his food to maximum benefit, and may have other serious repercussions. All horses should be wormed at least every six weeks.

Teeth. These must be rasped annually. The molars develop sharp edges as a result of wear. These sharp edges can affect a horse's ability to chew his food and may also lead to bit evasions.

These checks can be completed while the horse is still being kept at grass.

BRINGING THE HORSE UP FROM GRASS

Most competition and riding horses have a holiday, spending either some or all of the time at grass. Hunters have their break in the summer months and event horses tend to have their long rest in the winter. The duration of a horse's holidays depends upon the severity and pressure of his competitive career. A horse used for riding activities and gentle hacking will only need a short break from time to time, if he needs a rest at all. A horse who has hunted three times a fortnight for the whole season will benefit from a three month break at grass.

Assuming that the horse has been out at grass for some time, we shall discuss how to bring him up in preparation for a fitness programme.

Introduce stabling. Bring the horse in for a few hours daily to help him get used to being confined again. Always ensure there is ample fresh air by keeping the top door open. Use dust-free bedding and soaked hay to prevent coughing. Gradually increase the time he is stabled until he is being turned out for only a few hours a day.

Introduce exercise. Start by lungeing daily for ten minutes at walk to accustom the horse to being handled, gently stimulate heart and breathing rates and tone up the muscles.

Introduce short feed. While the horse is stabled he should have hay to prevent boredom. The amount will depend upon the type of horse and his condition. As work is introduced, he will need a small feed. Remember to introduce all changes gradually to allow the digestive system a period of adjustment and do not feed in excess of the amount of work being done. Also remember to stick to a routine — once the horse begins to have a daily feed you must ensure he has regular feed times.

Start grooming. The grass-kept horse can have minimal attention paid to him. His feet must be picked out daily and he can have a cursory brush over with a dandy brush. When he is to be excercised, the saddle and bridle areas must be clean to prevent chafeing. However, as he spends more time stabled, the grooming should be increased. He may also require clipping and trimming. If it is cold, he will need to be rugged up.

This programme of bringing the horse gradually from a grass-kept state to being stabled allows him a period of adjustment. It need not take very long and the amount of time taken will depend very much on individual circumstances. As an approximate guide, a fortnight should be adequate but the longer he has been on holiday, the longer the period of adjustment required.

A BASIC FITNESS PROGRAMME

WEEKS 1 AND 2
The horse will start off in 'soft' condition. His muscles lack tone, his lungs will be incapable of working to full capacity, his heart is not at its most efficient and he may be overweight.

All the early work should be done at walk, usually along the road. If there are suitable tracks to ride around, so much the better. Generally speaking, roads are not the safest of places but unfortunately, there is often no alternative.

Walk exercise increases the blood supply throughout the body, thus supplying all the muscles with oxygen. However, as the horse is not being subjected to excessive work he does not have to respire anaerobically and is therefore not likely to produce lactic acid. The gradual increase in circulation ensures that the muscles are warmed and oxygenated in preparation for the harder work to follow over the next few weeks. This preparation reduces the risk of injury, especially if carried out on a flat, level surface (rough, uneven ground should be avoided).

Initially thirty minutes a day will be enough but this should be gradually increased until, by the end of the second week, the horse is being walked for at least an hour a day. As the walking exercise progresses, so the fat is used up and the muscles begin to tone up and develop — note that fat is *not* converted into muscle. Ensure that the horse walks out actively and straight — he should not be allowed to dawdle.

When out hacking always use kneeboots as protection, in case the horse should stumble. If it is icy, use road studs to prevent slipping and an exercise sheet for warmth. Fluorescent clothing on both horse and rider will improve visibility, especially in the winter.

There are, it seems, exceptions to every rule and some horses, after an eight week holiday, feel extremely exuberant, making it unsafe to mount up and attempt to walk around the lanes. In such cases, it is better to lunge on a good surface and let the horse use up some energy without the rider on board. Change the rein regularly to reduce the risk of muscle or tendon strain. Once the horse has settled (and this may take several days) walk work can safely begin.

WEEKS 3 AND 4

Begin suppling work at walk in the school and introduce short spells of slow trotting. Approximately twenty minutes schooling before or after one hour's exercise, three times a week, should be sufficient.

The horse may be lunged two or three times a week, avoiding very small circles, which place strain on the limbs. Lunge sessions must be kept short — ten minutes initially building up to approximately twenty.

Introduce steady trotting on good going only and, if possible, slightly uphill. Once the horse is able to trot up a long slope without getting out of breath he may begin slow canter work.

WEEKS 5 AND 6

Short spells of canter are now introduced while schooling or out hacking — but avoid very hard or deep ground. Keep to good going only, to reduce the risk of concussion or strain. The horse may be keen to go faster than required but it must be remembered that his limbs, heart and wind are not yet ready; he must therefore be well restrained. If he is *very* fresh, it may be necessary to make temporary changes to tack. Do not canter on the lunge as the horse is not yet prepared for the extra strain this would exert.

It may be useful to enter a dressage competition to help gauge your schooling progress and give you an idea of what to work on at home. Gymnastic jumping may also begin — gridwork is an excellent means of suppling the horse.

WEEKS 7 AND 8
Four schooling sessions per week should be sufficient. This work can be made interesting by interspersing it with lungeing, gridwork and hacking.

The horse should now be ready to take part in a showjumping competition.

WEEKS 9 AND 10
The horse should now be starting to feel fairly fit. As an approximate guide, the canter work should, by now, have been built up to three sessions of three minutes with a break of three minutes walk between each. However, aim to canter not more than every fourth day. Excessive canter work is not necessary and leads to wear and tear on the joints and tendons.

Taking into account the factors which affect a horse's ability to achieve fitness, by the end of ten weeks fittening work the horse should be fit enough to compete in a BHS Novice Horse Trial. A couple more weeks will be needed if working towards an Intermediate or Advanced competition, because of the extra length of the courses and increased speeds.

Table 1 is a weekly fitness chart for working up to major three day event level. However, all such information must be used for guidance only — never be dogmatic when planning a fitness programme.

Table 1. A Sample Fitness Programme

	MONDAY	TUESDAY	WEDNESDAY	THURSDAY	FRIDAY	SATURDAY	SUNDAY
Weeks 1 & 2	Build up from 30 minutes walking daily to one hour						Rest
Week 3	Hack (walk) 1 hr	School 20 min Hack 1 hr	Hack 1 hr	School 20 min Hack 1 hr	Hack 1½ hr	School 20 min Hack 1 hr	Rest
Week 4	Hack 1¼ hr Introduce slow trot	Lunge 10 min Hack 45 min	School 20 min Hack 1 hr	Lunge 10 min School 20 min Hack 30 min	Hack 1½ hr Increase trot work	School 20 min Hack 1 hr	Rest
Week 5	Hack 1½ hr Trot 2 × 2 min 3 min walk in between	Lunge 10 min School 20 min Hack 30 min	School 30 min Hack 1 hr	As Tuesday	School 30 min Hack 1 hr Trot 3 × 2 min	Hack 1½ hr	Rest
Week 6	Lunge 15 min Hack 1¼ hr	School 45 min inc. gridwork Hack 30 min	Hack 1½ hr Trot 3 × 3 min	Lunge 15 min School 30 min Hack 30 min	As Monday Introduce short canter on hack	As Tuesday	Rest
Week 7	School 40 min Hack 1 hr	Hack 1½ hr Inc. trot 3 × 3 min Canter 2 × 3 min	School 45 min inc. gridwork Hack 30 min	Lunge 15 min School 30 min Hack 30 min	School 30 min Hack 1 hr Trot 3 × 3 min	Dressage Competition	Rest
Week 8	School 30 min Hack 1¼ hr	Hack inc. canter 2 × 3 min	Lunge 15 min School 30 min	School 45 min inc. gridwork	Showjumping Competition	Rest	Hack 1½ hr Canter 2 × 4 min
Week 9	School 30 min Hack 1¼ hr	Cross country Schooling Hack 30 min	School 30 min Hack 1 hr	Hack inc. canter 3 × 4 min	Hack 1½ hr	Showjumping Competition	Rest
Week 10	School 30 min Hack 1 hr inc. trot 3 × 3 min	Hack 1½ hr inc. canter 3 × 5 min @ 400 mpm 1 × 5 min @ 500 mpm	Hack 1½ hr Walk	School 30 min Hack 1 hr	School 45 min inc. gridwork Hack 45 min	One Day Event	Rest

Week							
Week 11	Hack 1½ hr / Walk	School 30 min / Hack 45 min	Hack inc. canter 3 × 6 min	Hack 1½ hr / Walk	School 45 min inc. gridwork / Hack 30 min	School 40 min / hack 1 hr	One Day Event
Week 12	Rest	Hack 1½ hr	School 40 min / Hack 1 hr	Canter (400 mpm) 2 × 6 min 1 × 7 min	School 30 min / Hack 1½ hr	School 40 min / Hack 1¼ hr	As Friday
Week 13	Rest	Hack 1½ hr	Canter (400 mpm) 3 × 7 min (last 3 min @ 500 mpm)	School 20 min / Hack 1½ hr	School 30 min / Hack 1½ hr	School 45 min inc. gridwork / Hack 1 hr	One Day Event
Week 14	Rest	Hack 1½ hr	School 30 min / Hack 1 hr	School 20 min / Canter 4 × 7 min	Hack 1½ hr	School 1 hr / Hack 1 hr	Rest
Week 15	School 45 min / Hack 45 min	Canter 3 × 8 min (last 4 min @ 500 mpm)	School 20 min / Hack 1 hr	School 45 min inc. gridwork / Hack 1 hr	School 30 min / Hack 1 hr	School 1 hr / Hack 30 min / Travel to Event	One Day Event
Week 16	Rest	School 30 min / Hack 1 hr	School 45 min / Hack 45 min	Canter 1 × 8 min @ 400 mpm, 1 × 8 min @ 500 mpm, 1 × 8 min @ 650 mpm	School 20 min / Hack 1 hr	School 40 min / Hack 45 min	Rest
Week 17	School 45 min inc. gridwork	Travel to Event / Hack 1 hr	School 1 hr / Hack 1 hr	Dressage work / Quiet hack 1 hr	Dressage	Speed and Endurance	Showjumping

INTERVAL TRAINING

There are certain top class trainers who rely purely on their experience, instinctive knowledge and 'feel' for their horses when fittening them for competition. However, for most people, a training programme provides an important framework around which to work whilst gaining valuable knowledge and experience, and many prefer the greater certainty of a 'scientific' approach.

Interval training is a technique which, if used with adequate preparation and planning, helps to take some of the guesswork out of getting a horse fit. Originally devised for use by human athletes, interval training consists of set work periods at a specified gait and speed, interspersed with set rest periods. During each walking rest period the horse is allowed to recover partially before being asked to work again.

Advantages

1) As the work periods are kept short, the risk of injury and fatigue is reduced.

2) The nature of interval training gradually increases the horse's tolerance of work, so reducing stress.

3) Interval training develops the horse's aerobic capacity.

4) Since the work periods are kept short the risk of lactic acid build-up as a result of anaerobic respiration is reduced. Furthermore, should any lactic acid be produced, the walk rest period allows its removal from the muscles via the bloodstream.

5) Close monitoring of the pulse and respiratory rates gives a positive and definite guide to the level of stress undergone by the horse.

6) Riding over the set distance in a set time helps to develop the rider's feel for speed and pacing.

Preparation

1) The horse needs to complete approximately four weeks' basic fitness work before commencing an interval training programme.

2) Take and record the horse's temperature, pulse and rate of respiration whilst at rest. It is a good idea to do this for a few consecutive days to gauge what is normal for each individual horse.

3) Find a suitable area, such as an all-weather gallop, long, wide verge or edge of a large field and measure a distance or distances of 400 m (440 yards). This measurement is to enable correct speeds to be calculated. Therefore, mark the start and finish of each 400 m section clearly.

4) Each 400 m section is to be covered in a set time, according to the speed required:

Time over 400 m	Speed mpm (metres per minute)
1 min 49 sec	220 mpm — brisk trot
1 min 4 sec	350 mpm — steady canter
1 min	400 mpm — slightly stronger canter
57 sec	425 mpm — strong canter

5) You will need a stopwatch to time yourself over the distance and for timing the pulse and respiratory rates.

6) Keep a record of your programme and the readings.

Beginning the programme

Start off with trot work in or around week five of the fitness programme. Warm up at walk for at least fifteen minutes. The following is an example of an initial session:

IT SESSION 1

1) Trot for two minutes at 220 mpm.

2) Walk for three minutes.

3) Trot for two minutes.

4) Halt and record pulse and respiratory rates.

5) Walk for ten minutes.

6) Halt and record pulse and respiratory rates.

If keeping a written record the above could be presented as:

IT SESSION 1

Date: / /					
1	2	3	4	5	6
(2)	3	(2)	Pulse: Resp:	10	Pulse: Resp:

Note: in Table 1 the above work session would be shown as 'Trot 2 × 2' (see Monday of Week 5).

Eventually, the trot can be built up and may be recorded thus:

IT SESSION 8*

Date: / /		
(3) 3 (3) 3 (3) 3 (3) Pulse: 10 Resp:		Pulse: Resp:

Trot periods should not exceed five minutes.

Obviously, all horses are different and will achieve fitness at different rates — the programme will have to be adjusted for individual horses.

When the horse is coping well with (recovering quickly from) the work-out shown in IT Session 8, the trot work can be increased. This is done by increasing the time but reducing the number, as below:

* The number 8 and subsequent numbers are used purely as examples.

IT SESSION 9

Date: / /
  (5)   3 (5)   3 (5)   Pulse: 10   Pulse:
                             Resp: Resp:

When the horse is coping well with Session 9, the canter work can be introduced. This may be recorded thus:

IT SESSION 10

Date: / /
Warm up for thirty minutes at walk and trot.
(canter at 350 mpm — minutes)
(1 min 4) 3 (1 min 4)   Pulse: 10   Pulse:
                        Resp: Resp:

Once the horse is coping well with this session, the canter can be built up:

---

  (3)   3   (3)   Pulse: 10   Pulse:
                       Resp: Resp:

Once he is recovering quickly from this session, the canter can be made slightly stronger:

(canter at 400 mpm — minutes)
  (3) 3   (3) 3   (3) Pulse: 10   Pulse:
                       Resp: Resp:

When the horse copes well with the above, recovering within the ten minutes, he should be fit enough to compete in a BHS Novice Horse Trial.

Terminology

The terminology of interval training is explained with reference to the sample table IT Session 1.

Recovery rate. Bringing the horse out of his stable and walking to the exercise area causes an increase in pulse and respiration in comparison to the resting rates. This increased rate must be noted, and is used as a base rate.

The recovery rate is the rate at which the circulatory and respiratory systems decrease from the working levels (recorded at 4 in the table), to base rate levels. The reading at 6 indicates how well the horse has recovered. For example, if back to base rate, he has recovered fully but, if rates are midway between 4 and base rate, he is only half recovered. These measurements can be used as a basis for estimating the level of fitness achieved.

Work intervals. 1 and 3 may be expressed as the work intervals. The number of work intervals per session are known as repetitions.

Training distance. A 400 m unit is the training distance. If using an all-weather gallop, it may be easier to use furlongs as a measurement. One furlong = one-eighth of a mile (approx. 200 m).

Training time. This is the time taken to cover the training distance. In our example, IT Session 1, the training time is 1 min 49 sec, resulting in a training speed of 220 mpm.

Relief intervals. The three minute walk at 2 is the relief interval. Once the horse has achieved a certain level of fitness the rider may choose to trot gently between canter work intervals. This is known as work relief. It has been proven in fitness trials that during steady trotting, the pulse and respiratory rates will lower very effectively and lactic acid will be removed from the system efficiently.

Recovery period. This is the ten minute walk period as specified in 5. It is the difference between the heart and respiratory rates taken at the beginning and end of this period that is referred to as the recovery rate.

When a horse is fit and finding each workout easy, he will recover within the ten minutes almost back to his base rates (he will not return *completely* to his 'at rest' rates because of the general stimulation of being out of the stable). Generally, a horse walking before any work has a heart rate of between 60 and 80 beats per minute.

As the horse gets fitter, so his recovery rate and level of recovery improve. The horse should *never* be overstressed. The amount of work is gradually increased by adding to the speed, distance and time and by using more demanding terrain, (slopes and hills), if possible.

Importance of monitoring the pulse rate

The pulse rate indicates the level of stress. The normal range of pulse rates at rest is between 35 and 42 beats per minute. If, after work, the horse has a pulse rate of:

100 beats per minute — he has not worked hard enough.

120 beats per minute — a good work level has been attained.

150 beats per minute — too much stress has been exerted.

200 beats per minute — the horse will be respiring anaerobically.

If the horse recovers well between readings 4 and 6 after IT Session 1, add a third 400 m trot to your next session. If he does not recover well, repeat IT Session 1 twice weekly and do not add more until the horse recovers in ten minutes.

Table 2. Approximate Heart Rates for Different Levels of Exercise

Activity	Heart rate (bpm)
Rest	35−42
Standing under tack	40−65
Walking	60−80
Slow trot	90−110
Fast trot	140−160
Canter	120−170
Gallop	160−200
Maximum/race speeds	205−240

Continuing the programme

Build up the trot work until the horse is trotting 5 × 400 m in approximately weeks 6 and 7. This must not be carried out more than twice a week — as a guide, interval training should take place every fourth day to allow complete recovery. During the intervening days the horse is schooled and hacked.

Points to remember

1) Without the pulse rates, progress cannot be monitored accurately. The rider can, however, judge the respiratory rate without dismounting.

2) The ground conditions will affect the programme; very deep going makes movement much harder work and increases the risk of injury.

3) Undulating, hilly ground also increases the stress factor.

4) Because of the above, be flexible and alter the programme as necessary to suit individual horses, ground conditions, etc.

5) Keep a written record of your programme for future reference.

6) Training sessions should be carried out at four-day intervals — never more frequently, but may be incorporated into the 'traditional' fittening programme.

Interval training to Advanced levels

Ideally, an Advanced horse will have reached the above-mentioned level of fitness approximately seven weeks before a major three day event that is, after six weeks of toning up and basic fittening. Some trainers advocate building up the work intervals to three sessions of ten minutes at 400 mpm and only introducing fast work in the last three weeks. It may prove too much for some horses to canter for three sessions of ten minutes at a stretch. In such cases, the training time is reduced and the speed slightly increased. Table 3 is an example of an interval training programme in the seven weeks leading up to a major three day event.

Table 3. The Latter Stages of an Interval Training Programme

Week 7	(Tues)	2 × 3 min at 400 mpm
Week 8	(Tues)	2 × 3 min at 400 mpm
	(Sun)	2 × 4 min at 400 mpm
Week 9	(Thurs)	3 × 4 min at 400 mpm
Week 10	(Tues)	3 × 5 min at 400 mpm
		1 × 5 min at 500 mpm
Week 11	(Wed)	3 × 6 min at 450 mpm
Week 12	(Thurs)	2 × 6 min at 400 mpm
		1 × 7 min:
		3 min at 400 mpm
		4 min at 500 mpm
Week 13	(Wed)	3 × 7 min:
		4 min at 400 mpm
		3 min at 400 mpm
Week 14	(Thurs)	4 × 7 min:
		3 min at 400 mpm
		4 min at 500 mpm
Week 15	(Tues)	3 × 8 min:
		3 min at 400 mpm
		5 min at 500 mpm

Note: some horses may be suited to shorter bursts of work, say 6 or 7 × 5 min instead. The trainer must judge each horse's programme individually.

Week 16	(Thurs)	1 × 8 min at 400 mpm
		1 × 8 min at 500 mpm
		1 × 8 min at 650 mpm

As mentioned above, 7 × 5 min with the last two minutes at 650 mpm may suit certain horses better than 3 × 8 min.

Week 17		Three Day Event

As previously discussed, it is impossible to write down an exact programme that would suit every horse, as each is unique in his ability to achieve fitness. Also, riders and trainers have access to varying standards of facilities — for example, some do not have a hill in their county, so to say 'you must include short bursts uphill' is rather futile.

In addition to treating each horse as an individual, the golden rules to be remembered are never overexert the horse and do not carry out interval training more frequently than at four-day intervals. (It may be necessary to work backwards from the date of a competition to decide the optimum days for canter work.)

The programme will have to be flexible enough to allow for adaptations when a continuing four-day cycle cannot be strictly adhered to, for example the training time, speed and number of repetitions may have to be reduced to prevent overstressing the limbs, heart etc. on the occasions when there are not three clear days between work-outs and competitions. This will inevitably occur when the horse is competing regularly on a weekly basis.

Fast work is only introduced in the last three weeks and should never be carried out 'flat out'. A three-quarter speed gallop over a distance of approximately 500 m (two and a half furlongs) will develop strength and speed whilst a longer, slower gallop of say half speed over 800 m (four furlongs) will develop endurance.

THE SPEEDTEST SYSTEM

This fittening programme has been adapted from a system used successfully by human athletes and may be tailored to meet the differing needs of the various types of competition horse. Basically, the speedtest system is a three stage programme. The length of the overall programme is dependent upon the horse's ability to achieve fitness (the influences of breeding, age, previous fitness etc.).

As with other fittening programmes, the first stage consists of a foundation of slow work. The first two weeks are spent at walk, after which trotting is introduced. The trot work is built up to approximately 3 km (2 miles) per day. This is built up further and canter work is introduced. Within this foundation stage, which may last approximately twelve weeks, the canter is built up so that on every third day the horse is cantered for approximately 10 km (6 miles). The work on the other two days should be easier and for a shorter duration.

The workload is determined on a four-week cycle — one week of moderate work, one hard, one moderate followed by an easy week. A heart rate monitor is used to ensure that the horse never becomes distressed. The duration of the canter periods will be determined by the horse's heart rate and the onset of fatigue — if the horse feels tired he must be allowed to rest and recover.

At the end of the three month period, short gallops are introduced. This is where the programme gains its other title, 'The Fartlek System' — fartlek is the Swedish word used to describe the short gallops. These gallops are run over a distance of between 200 and 600 m.

At this stage the heart rate monitor is invaluable for judging the degree of stress — if the heart rate goes too high the rider can slow down. An eventer is galloped for approximately one minute to push the heart rate up to 190–200 beats per minute. The horse is never galloped in easy weeks and never more than twice a week.

Before moving on to the second stage, a speedtest is used to assess the horse's level of fitness. The horse is galloped at a moderate speed over a distance of approximately 4 km ($2\frac{1}{4}$ miles). The heart rate is recorded and compared to previous readings. If the heart rate is low (around 160 beats per minute, followed by rapid recovery) the horse is fit enough to move on to the second stage.

The second stage lasts for approximately six weeks and is designed to develop further the respiratory and muscular structures. This involves increasing the fast work; an eventer may do a 3–5 km (2–3 mile) gallop, the speed of which is adapted to keep the heart rate below 180 beats per minute. This fast work is carried out twice a week, but never during a moderate or easy week. After approximately six weeks another speedtest is carried out over an increased distance.

At the third stage the competition conditions are simulated — the duration is decreased and the speed increased. A racehorse would be worked in intervals with gallops of about half a mile (just under 1 km) at racing pace, interspersed with trot work until the heart and respiratory rates have lowered. He would undergo such a test four days before a race.

An eventer is worked at speed over distances which are close to that of the level of the competition, for example, an Advanced horse would do three 1 km (five-furlong) gallops at steeplechase speed, while a Novice horse would work at Novice eventing speed over shorter distances.

The speedtest method of fittening is fairly flexible and provides variation throughout the programme, which helps to relieve boredom. It is, however, important that records are kept to gauge the horse's progress and that a great deal of common sense is used in determining whether the horse is becoming fatigued or not. If used properly by knowledgeable persons this system can achieve great fittening effects whilst avoiding the undesirable effects of fatigue.

ADDITIONAL TRAINING AIDS

Some yards have access to additional facilities such as horse-walkers, treadmills and swimming pools. All have advantages, the chief disadvantage being the cost involved.

Horsewalkers are particularly useful for warming up and cooling down a number of horses using minimal manpower. They are becoming increasingly popular in busy yards. One disadvantage of the horsewalker is the element of boredom. It is important that the facility to change direction is utilized, to avoid promoting 'onesidedness'.

Treadmills. These are not so popular as horsewalkers, but are useful for working one horse in bad weather or when ground conditions are adverse. The horse wears a harness and the treadmill is set at a specific speed. It can also be inclined up to ten degrees. The treadmill speed can be increased and used safely at speeds of up to 50 kph (30 mph). The harness prevents the horse from falling in the event of a power failure which may cause the treadmill to stop suddenly.

Swimming pools. Swimming provides a strenuous activity ideal for developing muscular and cardiopulmonary capacity. It is ideal for horses with joint and tendon problems as their limbs do not have to bear any weight, so exercise is given without the ill-effects of jarring. Swimming can also relieve the boredom of a stale, soured horse.

In order to further increase his heart rate the horse can be made to swim against a current.

All pools should have a safe ramp in and out. Some pools consist of a straight swimway only, whilst others are circular. Assistants have lines attached to a cavesson and are thus able to guide the horse through the pool safely.

MONITORING TO ASSESS FITNESS

The fitness requirements of each horse will differ with the level of competition — the trainer has to be able to judge when the optimum fitness level has been reached. It may be necessary to monitor the fitness level if the horse is not performing adequately. There are several different ways of doing this, some of which require specialist equipment and expertise.

Monitoring heart rate

Monitoring the heart rate is an accurate means of assessing fitness and may be done by the following methods:

Taking the pulse. This is done at a point where an artery passes over bone, close to the surface of the skin. The pulse is normally felt in the facial artery on the inner edge of the lower jawbone. Alternatively, the radial artery may be felt on the inside of the foreleg, level with the elbow.

Stethoscope. This is placed just behind the horse's left elbow. The stethoscope may be used by the rider/trainer to measure heart rate and is particularly useful when monitoring fitness.

Pulse monitor. Electrodes pressed onto the horse's skin record the heart rate. This can be read instantly by the rider on a digital display which is normally strapped to the wrist. These monitors are very useful when gauging the progress of fitness in the interval training programme.

Electrocardiogram (ECG). This specialized equipment used by the vet can measure and record the level of electrical activity created by the nervous impulses in the heart. The size of the heart can also be gauged as, the larger the heart, the longer it will take to contract.

A fit horse will have a slower resting heart rate, less increase in heart rate for any given amount of exercise and a quicker recovery rate.

Weight

Competition horses cannot perform properly if overweight. Observation is the method frequently used to assess weight gain or loss although it is better to be more precise by using a weighbridge or tape.

Racehorses have their optimum racing weight — some trainers weigh the horses before and after a race and are able to judge the degree of stress imposed upon the horse according to the amount of weight he has lost. Once the optimum racing weight has been determined, efforts are made to maintain it.

Gait analysis

The horse is filmed at all gaits and then, with the help of a computer, his action is analysed for efficiency and for any defects which may affect his future soundness.

Force plates

A 40×1.2 m track of hardwearing rubber containing many sensors is able to record all pressures exerted when a horse is walked or trotted on it. This sophisticated system was developed in Switzerland and is called the Kagi Gait Analysis System.

The vet or user of the force plates must be well trained in interpreting the readings. Print-outs of known sound and unsound horses are used as comparisons to the computer print-outs of each individual horse as an aid to diagnosis.

The main benefit of using this system as part of the fittening programme is that any abnormality of action which might be too slight to notice normally may be detected and can be investigated before a serious problem arises.

Thermography

This is another technique designed to detect areas of stress within the limbs before the problem becomes a serious one. An infra-red camera is used to record changes in temperature. Any area affected by wear and tear will undergo a rise in temperature before any signs of swelling are evident. If signs are found early enough, the necessary treatment or reductions in training intensity may well prevent the horse from becoming unsound during his fittening programme.

Determining the anaerobic threshold

While the horse respires aerobically, there will be little lactic acid production. However, the point at which the horse begins to respire anaerobically is identified by an increase in the quantity of lactic acid in the bloodstream. This point is known as the anaerobic threshold.

The anaerobic threshold will be determined by the horse's level of fitness; the fitter he is, the higher the threshold. The object of fittening a horse is to increase the aerobic capacity, thus delaying the point at which lactic acid is produced.

With the use of specialist machinery, it is possible to test the levels of lactic acid in the bloodstream. This is done before exercise commences to establish the normal 'at rest' levels. The horse is then worked at a specific speed for a set time, after which a blood sample is taken and lactate levels determined. This process continues until the anaerobic threshold is met.

An increase of lactic acid (acidosis) will occur when the blood-stream cannot remove it as quickly as it is produced. Lactic acid is produced by fast-twitch low oxidative (glycolytic) muscle fibres. The horse is tested throughout his training — once the threshold ceases to rise the horse is at the limit of his lactic acid tolerance, and has therefore reached his peak fitness.

If the threshold starts to fall it may be indicative of over-training or a relapse in fitness, possibly as a result of injury or illness.

The average trainer does not have the specialized equipment needed to measure the anaerobic threshold but, as a general guide, a horse who is showing a marked increase in respiratory rate after exercise will have respired anaerobically.

Blood and serum analysis

The various cells are present in the blood in characteristic proportions and analysis of these proportions helps to assess the state of a horse's health. To be of real benefit, tests must be taken regularly so that the normal proportions for the individual horse are known. The correct functioning of the organs and level of fitness of the horse may be tested through the analysis of a blood and serum sample in the laboratory. This is a specialist occupation undertaken by haematologists and bio-chemists. The results of their findings are interpreted by the veterinary surgeon. Depending upon the results, the diet and training programme can be adjusted as necessary.

In order to obtain a true reading, blood tests must be taken when the horse is at rest before exercise. This is because the spleen acts as a reservoir of blood, releasing this surplus into the system whenever it is under stress, for example, during exercise. The vet will insert a needle into the jugular vein and remove approximately 3 ml of blood, which is then mixed with an anticoagulant to prevent it from clotting. A further 6 ml (approx.) is taken and allowed to clot for serum examination. All blood must get to the laboratory within twenty-four hours as it starts to degenerate if kept too long. The absolute number of red and white cells can be determined by manual or sophisti-cated electronic means. The different types and proportions of white cells are determined either by a smear preparation or electronically. The remaining unclotted blood is then placed in a tube and spun at very high speeds (centrifuged) causing the cells to fall to the bottom of the tube. The proportion of blood cells to plasma may be measured as a percentage — this measurement is known as the packed cell volume (PCV). The normal range of PCV is between 34 and 44 per cent. The PCV gives a good indication of fitness and stress levels: if there is a very high percentage PCV, it indicates that the horse is highly excited, or suffering from dehydration and/or shock.

The blood cell levels are tested and recorded. Haematology is the study of blood cells; a haemagram used in fitness testing in horses may include the following counts:

RBC. Red blood cell count — the actual number of red blood cells per ml of blood.

Hb. The concentration of haemoglobin g/per ml blood. The haemoglobin in the red blood cells affects their oxygen-carrying capacity.

McV. The mean (average) red cell volume.

McHc. The mean (average) red cell haemoglobin concentration.

McH. The mean (average) red cell haemoglobin content.

WBC. White blood cell count. This is measured with an electronic cell counter. The different types of white blood cells are counted and the analysis is known as the differential WBC. The white cells (leucocytes) are concerned with the body's defence mechanism; a normal count indicates that the system is not under challenge.

PV. Plasma viscosity. The thickness of the blood is recorded thus. In conjunction with this, the erythrocyte sedimentation rate (ESR) is also recorded. In addition to indicating general unfitness, these two tests can lead to the detection of inflammatory conditions.

Serum biochemical tests

The fluid left after the blood has coagulated is serum — plasma minus the clotting agents. There are several serum tests used in fitness testing; as with haematology the biochemical tests are chosen selectively in accordance with specific requirements.

Serum proteins. These are albumins and globulins, the levels of which reflect nutritional balance and the efficiency of the digestive tract. Globulin levels tend to rise in response to disease.

Plasma electrolytes. These are the soluble mineral ions present in the plasma. Metabolism is dependent upon a balance of the various minerals.

Enzymes. Metabolism is also affected by enzymes — biochemical catalysts. If the metabolism is efficient the enzyme levels will be normal. The enzymes most often tested for are CPK, SGOT (AST) and Gamma GT.

CPK is an enzyme of the muscles and heart. Levels increase when azoturia and some cardiovascular conditions occur.

SGOT is found in all tissues. Its level in serum increases in response to azoturia, and some liver disorders.

Gamma GT is a liver enzyme which may increase gradually as training is built up. If the horse is overstressed the levels increase dramatically.

Conditions which may be monitored

Blood testing and serum analysis are expensive methods of gauging fitness so it is important that the trainer understands the vet's interpretation of the results and acts accordingly. Conditions which may show up through, and can be monitored by, this method include:

Anaemia. Shows as a lower red blood cell count and lower concentration of haemoglobin.

Azoturia. The severity of azoturia may be gauged by the levels of the enzymes creatine phosphokinase (CPK) and aspartate aminotransferase (AST) found in the muscles. Damage to muscle releases CPK and AST into the bloodstream.

Bacterial infection. The total number of white blood cells increases, as does the percentage of neutrophils.

Dehydration. The PCV percentage becomes higher because of loss of body fluid.

Fitness levels. With increasing fitness, the RBC count, PCV and haemoglobin levels increase.

Kidney function. Increased quantities of creatine and urea may indicate abnormal kidney function, as the kidneys normally excrete them.

Liver function. There are raised levels of various enzymes present when liver damage has occurred.

Muscle damage. This causes higher levels of CPK and AST (see Azoturia).

Parasitic damage. This is indicated by an increased quantity of beta globulin and a reduction of the blood protein albumin. Migrating worms damage the intestines and blood vessels, causing leakage and loss of albumin.

Viral infection. Typically, in acute viral infection, there is a reduction in the total number of white cells, and a reduced number of neutrophils in comparison to lymphocytes — the normal ratio of 60:40 (N:L) becomes 40:60. In the latter or recovery stages, an increase in total white cell count may be seen — this may be caused by bacterial secondary infection.

4

THE BACKGROUND
TO COMPETITION

While good preparation cannot make up for poor performance, it remains essential if horse and rider are to perform to the best of their ability, with the minimum of trauma and fuss. In this chapter, we will consider some areas where attention to detail — or the lack of it — can have considerable impact upon the success or failure of a competition venture.

TACK FOR THE DIFFERENT DISCIPLINES

The tack and equipment needed for the different types of competition varies but, whatever is used, it must be well maintained, clean, well fitting and safe. Below is a brief resumé of the type of equipment needed and permitted in the different disciplines, but always check the relevant (current) rule book! Rules on permitted tack and equipment may change from one year to the next.

Dressage (pure)

Bridle

Preliminary and Novice tests are to be ridden in a snaffle with either a cavesson, drop or flash noseband. Grackles are not permitted. Elementary and Medium tests may be ridden in a snaffle or simple double bridle, whilst all Advanced tests must be ridden in a double bridle.

Saddle and other equipment

This must be an English type saddle, although a purpose-built dressage saddle is not compulsory. The aim in dressage is (*very briefly!*), to shift the horse's centre of balance slightly backwards to encourage the hindquarters to carry a greater proportion of the weight, thus creating a lighter forehand and ultimately a degree of collection according to the standard of training of horse and rider.

The tree of the dressage saddle is shaped to follow the line of the horse's back, allowing the rider's weight to stay as close to the line of balance as possible. The seat is short, rarely exceeding 400 mm (16 in) and for this reason, the panels must distribute the weight evenly over as large an area as possible to avoid pressure points. The panels and flaps are straight cut to allow for a longer leg position, and the stirrup bars are set further back to encourage the leg to hang straight below the rider's body. The bars are recessed, fitted under instead of on top of the tree, to remove bulk from beneath the leg. Two elongated girth straps are used with the special, shortened, Lonsdale girth.

When choosing a dressage saddle, bear in mind that it should not put you into a drastically unnatural position, but must help you to sit in the centre of balance with an effective long leg. If you do not own a dressage saddle, a general purpose one is perfectly satisfactory for the lower levels of competition.

Boots, bandages and martingales are not permitted, although a hunting style breastplate is.

The dressage phase of horse trials

A steward is on hand to make a compulsory check of tack. This is normally done shortly before the dressage test. If, however, there is a chance that the horse may become upset by this (for example, resisting the steward's efforts to open his mouth to check the bit), you can request that the check be carried out afterwards. If, at this stage, the tack is found to be not as permitted, you will be eliminated.

Bridle

In Novice tests an ordinary snaffle must be used. This may be a straight bar or single or double jointed. If there are joints, all parts must be rounded and smooth. Rubber jointed snaffles are permitted. In Intermediate and Advanced tests a snaffle or simple double bridle may be used.

Nosebands permitted at all levels are the cavesson, drop, grackle and flash.

Saddle and other equipment

Regarding the saddle, the same points apply as for pure dressage. A breastplate or neckstrap is permitted. Martingales, running or draw reins, boots, bandages and blinkers are forbidden.

Showjumping (pure)

Bridle

For pure showjumping the rules are as laid down in the British Show Jumping Association's (BSJA) current rule book. In showjumping most bits, including hackamores, are permitted.

Saddle and other equipment

Use either a general purpose or forward-cut jumping saddle. The points of the jumping saddle slope forwards, enabling the stirrup bars to be attached further forward. This helps to keep the rider's weight over the horse's moving centre of gravity over a fence. The flaps are cut further forward to cover the panels. Most panels have knee rolls, some have thigh rolls as well, depending on personal taste. Some riders prefer less padding and a flatter seat to gain a greater 'feel' of the horse.

Martingales are allowed, as are Market Harboroughs. Boots and bandages are also permitted.

The showjumping phase of horse trials

Bridle

There are no limitations regarding bits however, if a martingale is worn, it must be either a running or Irish one. No blinkers, hoods, running reins or Market Harboroughs are allowed. On a fit, onward bound horse, it is advisable to use rubber-covered reins for extra grip.

Saddle and other equipment

As for BSJA jumping. The saddle must be black or tan in colour. It is safest to use a breastplate with a running martingale attachment, and an elasticated overgirth (surcingle) will hold the saddle securely in place. Boots, bandages and studs may be used as required.

Cross-country

The tack for the cross-country phase of a horse trial is much the same as for showjumping, but with the emphasis being firmly on safety, the following points should be borne in mind.

Bridle

Attach the headpiece of the bridle to the top plait, using a shoelace. This prevents the bridle from being pulled off over the horse's head in the event of a fall. Rubber reins with the buckle end knotted give good grip. The knot is helpful should you lose the reins, particularly down a drop fence.

Saddle and other equipment

If you are able to afford another specialist saddle there are special cross-country saddles on the market. However, most general purpose saddles are suitable for all jumping phases of a competition. Generally, a pair of webbing girths, with or without elastic inserts, are best for cross-country riding and rawhide stirrup leathers and stainless steel irons are strongest.

Always use an overgirth and a breastgirth or breastplate to prevent the saddle from shifting. An overgirth gives extra security if a girth strap breaks.

The breastgirth and breastplate in general use are:

The Aintree breastgirth. A webbing, elastic or leather strap passing round the front of the horse's chest, held in position by two straps which attach to the girth on either side and a single, adjustable strap which passes over the withers. The chest strap is often covered with sheepskin to prevent chafeing.

The hunting breastplate which consists of a leather strap which passes between the horse's forelegs and leads back to the girth, which passes through it. Attached to a ring at the breast is a V-shaped neckstrap which is attached by straps and buckles to the D-rings either side of the pommel. A running or standing martingale attachment may be fastened onto the breast ring.

Both are used to prevent the saddle from slipping sideways or backwards, particularly in competition circumstances and especially during the cross-country phase of a horse trial.

In Advanced One Day Horse Trials and all two and three day events, a minimum weight of 75 kg (11 st 11 lb) including the saddle must be carried. Lightweight riders will need to use a weight cloth beneath the saddle with the lead weights distributed evenly — mainly at the front to keep them in line with the centre of gravity. Check that the weight cloth does not rub and place it between the numnah and the saddle. Hooks can be used to suspend the cloth in the gullet of the saddle and prevent it from pressing on the spine.

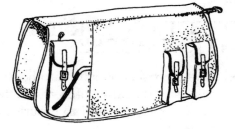

Figure 7 One type of cross-country weight cloth

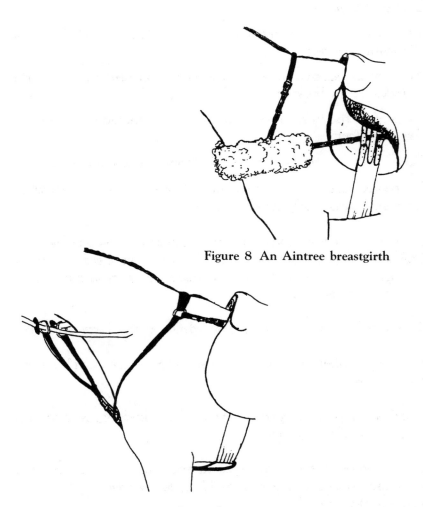

Figure 8 An Aintree breastgirth

Figure 9 A hunting breastplate

LEG PROTECTION FOR THE COMPETITION HORSE

Leg protection can be divided broadly into boots and bandages. All forms must be correctly and securely fitted, both in order to perform their functions properly and to ensure that they do not actually *cause* problems.

Types of boot

There are many different types of boot which are used for the following reasons:

To protect against knocks and blows on the inside of the fetlocks, as in brushing.

To protect the front tendons from injury inflicted by the toes of the hind feet.

To protect the bulbs of the heels from overreach injuries.

To protect the front of the cannon bone against knocks when jumping, particularly across country.

Some forms of boot offer support to the tendons whilst working and are easier to put on correctly than bandages. A lot of damage may be done by an inexperienced person putting on exercise bandages incorrectly.

Travelling boots offer protection whilst in the lorry or trailer.

Knee boots offer protection against injury whilst travelling and hacking out.

Hock boots protect against rubs whilst travelling, and against capped hocks in the stable.

Poultice boots are extremely useful when dealing with puncture or bruise wounds to the sole, holding the poultice in place and keeping the foot clean.

Working boots

Brushing boots

Brushing may occur in a young, green horse whose balance or rhythm is not yet established. Injuries may occur particularly when working on the lunge. It may also result from bad conformation and action, faulty shoeing or weakness and fatigue. The introduction of lateral work may also produce intermittent brushing and it is good practice to protect all horses when teaching such movements. Indeed, to prevent injury, all horses should be booted up for work.

Brushing boots may be made of synthetic materials such as rubber, which usually have Velcro fastenings. These are very quick and easy to put on. If Velcro-fastened boots are used for minor cross-country competitions, wind electrical tape around the top and bottom to help keep them in place. Some synthetic boots have fleecy linings and elasticated hook attachments for fastenings. Check that the elasticated straps are not done up too tightly.

The most durable boots are leather with fleecy linings and strap and buckle fastenings. These must be kept clean and supple to prevent sores; boots which rub can cause dreadful injuries that will scar the legs. The fleecy lining and padding will wear out before the boot does, so will have to be replaced by a saddler.

Hind boots are longer than front boots and have at least one extra strap. The top and bottom straps should not be fastened too tightly or they will interfere with the flexion of the fetlock joint, cause pressure ridges and trap dirt and grit. Fasten the centre strap first, then the top, leaving the lower ones until last. When removing the boots, undo the buckles in the reverse order.

Fetlock boots

These are made from the same materials as brushing boots, but cover only the fetlock joint. They are popular with showjumpers for use on the hind legs as the horse can feel the discomfort if he hits a pole, but his fetlocks are protected against brushing when turning.

Speedy-cut boots

High brushing is known as speedy-cutting, so named because this type of injury occurs mainly at speed. The boots for protection are longer than normal brushing boots.

Polo boots

These are longer than brushing boots, are very strong and cover as much of the horse's lower leg as possible. The hind boots have an extra-low flap for protection. In some polo boots, strong elastic is built in for tendon support.

Yorkshire boots

These are made simply from a rectangle of material, normally felt, with a tape sewn along the centre. The tape is tied just above the fetlock joint and the top half of the rectangle is folded down over the lower half, giving two layers of protection. These boots do not usually wear very well but can made cheaply and easily.

Fetlock ring boot

This hollow rubber ring fits over the fetlock and acts as a buffer against brushing, but offers no additional support or protection.

Tendon boots

These are open at the front, but offer support and protection to the tendons. They are used by showjumpers because, as with fetlock boots, the horse can still feel some discomfort if he hits a pole, but the tendons are protected. They are made from leather or plastic and are normally used only on the front legs.

Overreach boots

Overreaching may occur when a short-backed horse with engaged hindquarters strikes the bulb of a forefoot with the toe of a hind or otherwise, when a horse is jumping or galloping.

Overreach boots are normally made of rubber, with or without strap fastenings. The bell boots without straps are turned inside out, stretched on over the hoof and then pulled down the right way. This can be very difficult on a horse with big feet! The buckle type of boot is easier to put on but is more prone to tearing off while the horse is in action.

Many people refuse to use overreach boots for cross-country because of the risk of the horse treading on the boot with a hind toe and falling. Overreach boots also have a tendency to flip up in use. Leather overreach boots, sometimes called coronet boots, offer excellent protection and do not flip up. They must, however, be kept clean and supple, with a close eye being kept on the pastern and coronet for signs of rubbing.

Knee boots

The injury referred to as 'broken knees' can range from a superficial scratch to a deep injury causing puncturing of the joint sac with loss of synovial fluid. It can be caused by:

The horse stumbling up or down the ramp when being loaded or unloaded from the lorry.

The horse stumbling on the road whilst out hacking.

Hitting a fence very hard in front.

Knee injuries are very slow to heal because of the joint flexion, and nearly always cause scarring. To prevent them there are two types of kneeboot; the plain one, which is used mainly for travelling and the skeleton kneeboot, which is less cumbersome than the plain one and thus commonly used for exercise.

The buckles fasten on the outside, with the ends of the straps pointing forwards. The top, elasticated, strap is fastened first, quite firmly. The lower strap is fastened last, very loosely, to allow joint flexion.

When removing kneeboots always undo the lower strap first. If the top strap is undone first the boot may slip down and become entangled around the foot.

Disadvantages of working in boots

Despite the protection they offer, there are potential drawbacks to working in boots. Bearing these in mind when choosing and fitting boots will help prevent their occurrence:

Synthetic linings may cause sweating, irritation and an inflammatory reaction.

Ill-fitting, old or worn boots, particularly leather, will rub.

Dirt and grit may be trapped between the boot and the skin, causing irritation.

Horses may tread on rubber overreach boots which also have the tendency to flip up or be torn off and lost during competition.

Boots which are fastened too tightly and/or left on for too long will restrict circulation and may cause bruising and pressure sores.

Boots do not generally offer the same degree of support as bandages.

Other boots

Hock boots

Thick felt boots with padding and two leather straps. The straps are buckled in the same manner as knee boots, except that the ends of the straps normally point backwards.

Sausage boot

Similar in concept to the fetlock ring boot, this is a thickly padded leather circle which fits around the pastern to prevent

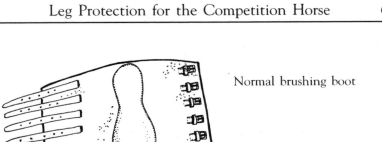

Normal brushing boot

Overreach boot

Speedy-cut boot

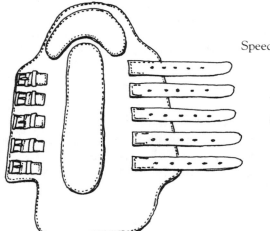

Plain knee boot

Figure 10 Types of working boots

the horse from capping his elbow with the heel of his shoe when lying down in the stable.

Travelling boots

These are thickly padded boots which are long enough to protect the knee or hock and coronets. They are very quick and easy to put on but can be prone to slipping down if not fastened securely.

Poultice boots

These may be made from leather, canvas or rubber and fit over the whole foot, with straps and buckles to draw the boot securely around the hoof, holding a poultice dressing in place. The advantage of these over the traditional method of using bandages and sacking to hold a foot poultice in place is that, with the latter, the sack wears through and absorbs moisture from the bedding. The disadvantage of poultice boots is that they may cause sores around the coronet.

Equiboot

This strong boot fits exactly over the hoof. It can be adjusted at the heel to ensure that it is neither too loose nor too tight. The Equiboot is used to protect the foot if the horse cannot be shod but is required to work, and can also be used to hold a poultice or dressing in position.

Bandages

Stable bandages

These have several uses:

1) They improve the circulation and reduce puffiness so may be of benefit to the working horse whose limbs show signs of wear and tear. Especially after competing or jumping on hard ground, wash the legs in a diluted cooling lotion and

bandage to help keep any swelling to a minimum. Check legwash directions for any contra-indications; in some cases it is not advisable to bandage over neat cooling gel or liniment. Examine the legs daily and note any changes. When applying stable bandages to prevent filling, start to apply the bandage at the bottom of the leg and bandage upwards to assist in dispersal of fluid.

2) They may be used to help hold a dressing in place and prevent the horse from interfering with the dressing.

3) They can be used in the stable to provide warmth for a sick or cold horse (never close the top door to keep a horse warm). Remove the bandages every twelve hours and massage the legs before replacing.

4) They may be used to dry off the legs after washing.

Exercise bandages

These offer protection against blows, and support to the tendons, which is particularly needed when jumping. Many people advocate their use only when jumping on hard ground or in deep, holding conditions. However, horses prone to tendon injury will generally benefit from the support offered by correctly applied exercise bandages.

Exercise bandages must be applied by one person per horse to ensure an even tension on each leg. When used in competition, stitch with a darning needle or wrap electrical tape around the top and bottom. Stitching is the safer method, being less likely to cause uneven pressure; electrical tape does not give with the bandage. Stitch the bandages using large cross stitches (X-shaped).

Exercise bandages may also be used over tendon protectors. These consist of a double thickness of Plastazote which is moulded to the shape of the leg, is light and will not retain water. Some forms of tendon protector have a strip of impact-resistant polythene running down the back between the two Plastazote layers, offering greater protection. For added protection behind, use tendon protectors under brushing or speedy-cut boots, with the toughened strip running down the front of the cannon bone.

Dressage horses are often worked in soft, wide bandages so that the legs are supported and protected whilst not being irritated by the stiffer boot materials.

Support bandages

Sometimes called pressure bandages, these are used in the stable to give support and to relieve swelling. They are made from stockinette and used over gamgee or Fyba-tack. Both legs must be bandaged to offer support to the sound leg also, as this will be bearing more weight. The bandage must extend down to the coronet to prevent filling. Unless otherwise directed by the vet, remove at least every twelve hours and massage the leg before re-applying.

PREPARING FOR A COMPETITION

Every event, whether an international competition or a local event, requires organized preparation. Obviously the higher the level of competition, the longer the stay away, and the more horses competing, the more thorough this preparation has to be. Depending upon the type and level of competition, the fitness programme will have started some twelve to sixteen weeks earlier. Correct training and a high standard of stable management should ensure that the horse is physically and mentally prepared for his events.

As the competition draws near, so the trainer must assess the horse's level of fitness and training. In the lead up to a one day event the horse should compete in dressage, showjumping and cross-country competitions. In preparation for a three day event the horse must compete in a specified number of one day events at a suitable level and complete the cross-country phase without jumping penalties. The qualifying requirements for the various competitions are laid out in the relevant rule books.

The week before

The stable and work routine should continue as normal. The shoes should be checked, making sure that the stud holes have a good thread. Once cleaned out these should be plugged with oily cotton wool. Check the spare set of shoes also. All tack and equipment must be checked so that any emergency repairs can be carried out. The competition list must be checked to ensure that everything is available and in clean, safe order.

Re-clip the horse if necessary, trim up and pull the mane and tail. Nearer the day of departure, give the horse a bath — if weather permits.

Check the horsebox, or car and trailer. Any problems may then be sorted out in the intervening days. If the weather has been particularly cold and a lorry has been standing, it may be reluctant to start. It is better to find out in advance so that the battery can be charged up.

The day before

1) Pack the lorry with all necessary equipment. Check that gear which 'lives' in the lorry has not been removed. Pack everything neatly into wicker baskets, cupboards or shelves.

2) Plan your journey, allowing extra time for fuel stops, and unexpected delays (punctures etc.).

3) Ring for times (unless at a three day event, in which case times will be posted at the event). Write the times down carefully twice — stick one copy up in the lorry and keep a spare copy on your person.

Competition lists

The following are lists of items likely to be needed at a horse trial. This can be modified to suit the requirements of other competitions.

Horse management list

Stable equipment
Fork.
Shovel.
Broom.
Skip/barrow.
Haynets (2).
Water buckets (2).
Feed bowl.
Bucket for soaking pulp, if fed.
Tub/plastic dustbin for soaking hay.
Feed scoop.
Two large water containers, full.

Feed
Hay.
Short feed as necessary.
Supplements.
Salt.
Electrolytes.

Grooming equipment
Complete grooming kit in easy-to-carry box.
Several sponges.
Clippers and blades — useful if away for more than a few days, especially if competing in a hot climate.
Plaiting kit and box or steps to stand on.
Studs, stud tap, spanner, cotton wool.
Spare set of shoes with studs fitted.
Correct size shoeing nails.
Hoof oil.
Bucket and sweat scraper for washing horse down.
Old towels.
Chalk whitener.
Baby oil.

Horse clothing
Waterproof sheet.
Exercise sheet.
Stable rugs and rollers.
Thermatex/anti-sweat sheets.
Summer sheet.
Spare woollen day rug.
Elasticated surcingle.

Spare stable bandages.
Exercise bandages.
Gamgee/Fyba-tack.
Spare headcollar and leadrope.

Tack and equipment list

Dressage phase
Horse
Snaffle bridle — drop, cavesson, flash or grackle (horse trials only) noseband or double bridle — cavesson noseband.
Black rubber-covered reins.
Dressage saddle and Lonsdale girth.
GP saddle and normal leather girth.
Stirrup irons and leathers.
White numnah.
Breastplate if needed.
Studs according to ground conditions.

Rider
Number bib — needed for all phases.
Beige breeches.
Tweed/navy/black jacket (may be tails if Intermediate or higher — gentlemen may wear red — check relevant rule book).
Top hat (with tails) or navy/black hat or crash cap cover (chin fastening not compulsory).
Black boots (see relevant rule book re. brown tops on black boots for gentlemen — must be worn with white breeches).
Gloves.
Spurs.
Schooling whip — *not* carried during horse trials test but may be carried for warming up if needed.
Shirt.
Coloured stock (with tweed jacket).
White stock (with navy/black jacket).
Stock pin.
Hairnet (ladies).

Showjumping phase
Horse
Jumping or GP saddle.
Numnah.
Girth.
Overgirth (surcingle).
Rawhide leathers (pre-stretched).
Stainless steel irons.
Optional type of bit as required.
Rubber-covered reins.
Running martingale or breastplate and martingale attachment.
Rein stops.
Studs according to ground conditions.
Brushing boots or exercise bandages.
Overreach boots.
Electrical tape to fasten bandages (must be stitched first).

Rider
Beige breeches ⎱
Boots   ⎰ as dressage.
Tweed/navy/black jacket.
Crash cap with navy or black cover.
Hairnet (ladies).
Gloves.
Coloured/white stock depending upon colour of jacket.
Stock pin.
Spurs — with blunted ends to point downwards.
Whip — not to exceed 0.75 m (30 in).

Cross-country phase
Horse
Tack as for showjumping.
Pair of webbing cross-country girths with elasticated inserts.
Weight cloth ⎱
Lead   ⎰ if needed.
Numnah.
Studs in accordance with ground conditions.
Shoelace passing through headpiece and top plait, secured to prevent bridle being pulled off.

Rider

Cross-country sweater and matching silk.   Gloves.
Boots and breeches as for showjumping.   Spurs.
Stock but no stock pin.
Back protector.
Crash cap.
Whip.
Stopwatch (and spare).
Medical card and armband holder.
Number 6:6.

Miscellaneous

Vaccination certificates/passports (essential at official competitions).
Road map.
Rule book.
Schedule and competitors' information.
Copy of dressage test.
Vehicle passes.
Stable passes.
Money.
Wet weather clothing − hat, wellies, wax jacket.
Hot weather clothing − sunglasses, shorts, T-shirts, trainers, sun tan lotion.
Complete change of jeans, jumpers etc.
Smart clothes if attending event drinks party.
Toiletries.
Basic provisions − tea, milk, biscuits etc.
Lungeing cavesson and rein.
Side reins.
Lunge whip.
Spare reins, girths and stirrup leathers.
Tack cleaning equipment.
Pincers for emergency shoe removal.
Hole punch.
If taking a dog a lead, bedding and food.

Everything will need to be checked for safety, thoroughly cleaned and packed into chests/hampers.

First aid kits
Horse
Electrolyte powders.
Eventing leg grease and rubber gloves.
Vaseline.
Animalintex and kaolin poultices.
Epsom salts.
Normal salt.
Wound powder/cream.
Cotton wool.
Gamgee.
Assorted bandages.
Tendon cooling lotion/gel or Ice-tight.
Muscle liniment.
Scissors.
Lint.
Waterproof sticking plaster.
Fly repellent.
Thermometer

Human
Pre-packed first aid kit, which is kept in the lorry at all times.

5

THE COMPETITIONS

HORSE TRIALS

The information given below relates specifically to a major horse trial (three day event). The general principles, however, especially those regarding preparation, planning and care of the horse, are equally relevant to lesser levels of competition. Information regarding the cross-country phase will be useful to riders participating in hunter trials.

Preliminaries

If riding in a three day event it is a good idea to arrive, if possible, on the Tuesday afternoon if the first day of dressage is on the Thursday. This gives the horse a chance to settle into his stable and become accustomed to the surroundings before the competition begins. A quiet hack out will familiarize both horse and rider with the layout of the area.

The competitors' briefing is generally held on the Wednesday and must not be missed. Programmes will be given out, along with maps of the speed and endurance phase. Now is the time to ask questions and generally find out what the format of the next four days is to be.

The grooms should attend the briefing and go on the drive round the roads and tracks phase which follows. It is important that the grooms are aware of the starting areas for the different phases and in which areas the rider is allowed assistance.

While driving around phases A and C (the roads and tracks), it is important to note all direction markers, checkpoints, kilometre signs and any other landmarks which can be used to assess your whereabouts. The grooms need to work out the quickest route from the start of one phase to the start of the next, bearing in mind that on the day of the speed and endurance there will be spectators and rough terrain to contend with. A four-wheel drive vehicle is very useful for this purpose.

Phase B, the steeplechase, is walked carefully, noting the exact quarter, halfway and three-quarter points for the calculation of timings. Usually the steeplechase consists of five fences on a loop, each fence being jumped twice. Some courses have a slightly more complicated arrangement and great care is needed at gallop to ensure that you do not go the wrong way.

Phase D, the cross-country course, is walked three or four times (not all in the same day!) so that the rider knows exactly which route to take from the moment of leaving the start box.

The horse will need to be exercised in the areas permitted. There are often white-boarded dressage arenas set up for schooling purposes.

The first inspection

The first veterinary inspection is held in the late afternoon before the first day of dressage and, for this, the horse should be immaculately turned out and plaited, led by an equally smart rider. Lead the horse around for approximately half an hour before the inspection to settle and loosen him. During this time, keep protective boots on the horse and, at the last minute, remove them and brush any small stones out of the feet.

The dressage phase

On the day of the test plan the horse's exercise and working-in programme so that the grooms know when you need to be mounted and which tack you require. Allow ample time for warming up and smartening up — both horse and rider should be turned out to the highest standard. Hopefully, a calm and polished test will follow.

Once the dressage test is over, the tack may be changed and the horse taken for a 'pipe-opener' (a fast canter to increase respiratory and heart rates) in preparation for the speed and endurance phase the next day.

Preparation for the speed and endurance phases

Later in the day after the dressage test, the cross-country course can be walked again and the exact time schedule for the four speed and endurance phases calculated, using the optimum times.

Phase A — roads and tracks — gives you your start time. There will be a set distance to be covered in a certain number of minutes, so work out at what time you should pass each kilometre marker and arrive at the finish of Phase A.

Before Phase B, the steeplechase, there will be a few minutes at the holding area for tack adjustments and, if needed, a farrier should be present.

There is a set time in which the steeplechase must be completed if you are to avoid time penalties. Calculate exactly when this will start and finish if you are travelling at the correct speed. Walking the course once more with a measuring wheel will enable you to determine the quarter, half and three-quarter points. If skilful enough, you may be able to check your watch at these points, to determine whether you are going at the correct speed.

Having finished Phase B you will enter a 'dead area' where grooms may attend to you or the horse if necessary. Ideally, you should keep going and set straight out onto Phase C to avoid wasting time.

For this, the second roads and tracks, note your intended start time and the time at which you plan to pass each kilometre marker, bearing in mind that you may wish to walk the first three-quarters of a kilometre to allow the horse to regain his breath. Phase C finishes as horse and rider enter the ten minute halt box at the start of Phase D.

During this halt, which is compulsory, grooms may attend to horse and rider. Your start and finish times for Phase D should be calculated using the official optimum time. This, together with relevant distances and speeds, will be set out in the programme. All three factors will vary depending upon the level of the competition.

Using the official times given, write out all calculations clearly on a square card and make copies; one to be taped to your arm, one spare for your pocket and another to be given to the grooms. On the morning of the event, make sure that the grooms have a stopwatch which, like your own, is synchronized to the event's official timing system.

Check all the tack and equipment that will be needed for the following day and get everything ready. The feed given on the evening before the speed and endurance phases should be normal, although no hay should be given after about 9 p.m. The horse should be bedded down on non-edible bedding so that he does not fill his intestines with bulk.

Riding the speed and endurance phases

In the morning, give only a small short feed and no hay unless the horse is starting very late in the day. In this instance he may have about $\frac{1}{2}-1$ kg (1−2 lb) of hay only. It is important not to remove the water bucket − the horse is unlikely to take a long drink prior to leaving his stable if he has had constant access to water.

Heavy rain overnight may have altered the going on the course, making it deep and/or slippery. It may be necessary to walk out onto the course and check the more difficult fences again. Once the competition has started you may have the opportunity to see how the other riders are tackling the course − unless you are one of the early competitors yourself.

Ensure everything is ready for the horse's return to the stable after the competition. As your start time draws near, your horse can be tacked up and led to the start of Phase A. Here you will weigh in when asked to do so by the stewards. Check that all tack, boots etc. are correctly fitted and then mount up. Ask the timer for the exact length of time to go before you start. Check girths and surcingle and check your stopwatch. (There are various different types of stopwatch available, with different functions. It is a good idea to have a spare watch strapped to your arm as an extra safeguard.) Whichever type of watch you use, it must be easy to operate and read, and be synchronized to the event's official timing. There is normally a master clock at the start of Phase A. Your timing calculations must be taped securely to your arm — make sure the ink is protected from water. The card may be neatly placed in a small plastic bag for protection.

Once you have mounted, the rug can be pulled off the horse's hindquarters and he can be walked quietly around. Phase A acts as a warm-up for Phase B; set off at a brisk trot. Once you are on your way, the team of helpers must drive to the start of Phase B. If possible, finish Phase A with a couple of minutes in hand. At this point the horse should not be blowing, but in extreme hot and humid weather conditions it may be necessary to cool him by sponging him with cold water, then scraping off. Also, allow him a small drink, if he wishes.

Before you begin Phase B, the stirrups will need to be shortened and all tack checked. Start the steeplechase at a steady gallop and try to settle into a rhythm. Check your watch at the designated marker points to help assess your speed. (If your horse lacks speed, do not press him *too* hard in an effort to achieve the optimum time on this phase, as this will be detrimental to his performance across country. Similarly, on the cross-country phase, consider your horse's limitations; do not set off too fast and risk finding yourself tackling the last part of the course on an overtired horse.)

Once the steeplechase is over, continue on through the 'dead area'. Your assistants should be there to check the horse's shoes and soundness as you walk or trot past. If all is going well, it is better not to stop here although, if it is very hot, cold water sponging is advisable, as is a sip of water. Equipment which must be on hand in case of need at the end of phase B consists of:

Bucket.
Water.
Sponges and scrapers.
Bag of ice, or ice pack* wrapped in cloth.
Spare bridle, girths, leathers, irons, stopwatch, stick and set of shoes (studs fitted).
Energy drink for rider.
First aid essentials.
Hole punch.
Equiboot (for use on Phase C if a shoe is lost on Phase B and no farrier is immediately available).

Generally, the first section of Phase C is ridden at a walk to allow the horse and rider to regain their breath. After this, some riders alternate between walk and canter while others maintain a regular, brisk trot. Each horse is different, so no hard and fast rules can be set. It is also permissible to dismount and lead the horse. The rider must weigh up the advantages and disadvantages of this but *must* be mounted when passing through the finish of Phase C. While the rider is on Phase C, the assistants must get to the compulsory ten minute halt box at the start of Phase D. Equipment needed in the halt box consists of:

Buckets (3).
Water containers — 1 plain cold water, 1 plain hot water.
Glucose powder.
Several towels.
Several sponges.
Sweat scrapers.
Ice packs (if weather conditions are very hot and/or humid).
Sweat sheet/cooler rug.
Thermometer.
Spare set of shoes with studs fitted.
Stud box including stud tap, spanner and studs.
Vaseline or leg grease and rubber gloves.

* The rider may also wish to take the ice pack onto Phase C to use to cool the horse further by holding it over his poll and rubbing it over his neck.

Antibiotic powder/spray.
Plaiting kit (bandages may need re-stitching).
Electrical tape.
Hole punch.
Headcollar and rope.
Spare reins, whip, girth, surcingle, boots, bandages, stirrup
leathers, saddle and bridle.
Different bit, if necessary.
Programme and course plan.
The rider will need an energy drink and sweets, dry gloves, and
a jacket to prevent chilling.

At the finish of Phase C, the horse should trot into the box
so that the veterinary panel can inspect him for soundness.
If the panel feel he looks distressed they will take the pulse
and respiratory rates, at the start and finish of the ten
minute break. If the horse is not fit to continue they will insist
that he is withdrawn. Once the veterinary panel has finished
looking at the horse (if all is well, this only takes a minute at
the most), the rider may hand the horse over to the grooms.
One should hold the horse while at least two others work
on him. He should stand facing into the breeze to help
him regain his breath, and in the shade if conditions are
hot. In humid conditions, fans should be available to assist
cooling.

Folded towels are tied above the knees and hocks so that
water from the washing down does not soak the boots or
bandages. The noseband may be undone, girths loosened and
the saddle lifted up and forwards to allow his back to dry. The
horse's mouth is washed out and his body washed as necessary.
Cold water helps to cool the body (or *iced* water, in hot, humid
conditions). This water must be scraped off immediately to aid
cooling. (Heat is transferred from the body to the water. Scraping
the water off 'removes' heat and allows further evaporation
from the surface of the skin.)

However, in very hot conditions, ice packs can be held over
the top of the horse's head, down his neck and between the hind
legs to cool the blood and cold water, to which ice cubes have

been added, used for washing off. Particular attention should be paid to the areas where the blood vessels are closest to the surface of the skin. He must then be scraped. Take care not to stand the horse still for too long — locomotion aids removal of lactic acid from the muscles. Once the washing down procedure is complete and the towels have been removed from his legs, the horse may be led about quietly.

An appropriate rug is put on and shoes and studs checked. Larger studs may be needed than were used on the roads and tracks. A farrier is available in the box to replace any shoes as needed.

The rider must be free to have a drink and talk to the trainer about the way in which the course is riding.

If necessary the bit can be changed and boots or bandages adjusted as necessary.

Approximately three minutes before the start time, the saddle is replaced and girths tightened. The noseband must be re-fastened. All water is wiped from the reins and stirrup irons and mud wiped off the rider's boots. The rider is then legged on.

Grease is spread on the front of the horse's legs by an assistant wearing rubber gloves — these will prevent a groom who subsequently handles the tack from making it slippery. The grease helps the horse to slide rather than cut himself or fall if he hits a fence, but it must not touch the tack.

A groom then checks the girths again and if the horse is to be led into the start box, passes a lead rope through either one or both bit rings. The horse is led into the start box at the correct time and, when instructed to do so by the rider, the groom slips the rope out of the bit rings. (The rope should never be clipped on as it is very difficult to undo under stress, particularly when the horse is getting excited.)

While the procedure described is the essence of what goes on in the halt box, every rider and team have a tried and tested routine on speed and endurance day — every horse is different and every rider has a preferred method of doing things.

Once the horse and rider are away on Phase D the team must prepare for their return at the finish area.

After-care of the horse

Hopefully, the horse will come through the finish of the cross-country at a strong pace, working up to the rein contact. The rider will then walk and dismount. At a major event the stewards will hold the horse while the rider weighs in. In the case of a lightweight rider, the weight of the saddle, weight cloth and lead is taken into account. If necessary, the bridle and martingale can also be weighed. If still under weight, the penalty is elimination. No-one other than an official steward may hold the horse while the rider removes the saddle. The penalty for a mistake at this point is elimination.

Once weighing-in is completed the grooms may take the horse. A cooler rug or anti-sweat sheet must be put on, with an extra blanket or waterproof sheet, depending on the weather. If the saddle is still on, the girths are loosened but the saddle should not be removed immediately. The horse must than be walked around for approximately five to ten minutes. Depending upon the geography of the site, the walk back to the stables may give the horse time to recover.

While the horse is walking around, the circulatory system removes lactic acid from the muscles, so helping to prevent 'tying up'. Walking also creates a current of air which helps cool the horse.

The temperature, pulse and respiratory rates (TPR) should be checked to ascertain how far above normal they are. Note how the horse is breathing — deep breaths indicate that he is inspiring more oxygen, whereas shallow, rapid breaths are taken if the horse is trying to cool down — an indication that he may be overheated. TPR rates should be checked again after a further fifteen minutes by which time they should be near normal.

While the horse is being walked, the weather conditions must be considered. For example, if it is very hot, keep the horse walking in the shade and, if it is very cold and windy, try to walk in a sheltered area.

Washing down

Once his breathing has returned to near normal, the horse can be thoroughly washed down. If the horse has a body temperature of between 41 and 43 °C (104 and 106 °F) and the weather is hot and humid, he must be cooled rapidly, as mentioned earlier. Icy water can be used on areas where arteries run close to the surface of the skin, for example between the hind legs, under the tail and on the face. Ice packs held at the poll and along the spinal column will cool the main organs of the central nervous system, the brain and spinal cord. Ice packs or icy water may be applied to the whole body *provided that the horse is kept walking* — icy water causes blood vessels to constrict and can lead to 'tying up' if the horse is allowed to stand still for too long.

If the horse is visibly distressed he must be led around whilst another assistant sponges him down.

All water must then be scraped off the body to facilitate effective cooling, and the horse is then led around, suitably rugged if necessary, to aid drying.

In hot, humid conditions a fan is very useful for cooling down — moving air currents will take away the heat lost through evaporation.

During the cooling process the horse should be allowed to take 'chilled' water — water that has had the chill removed — ad lib. Offer two buckets of water — one containing an electrolyte solution, one without. The horse can then satisfy his own requirements. Once fully recovered, he can be allowed to graze in hand.

Leg care

Scrape off the leg grease using a blunt knife and wash thoroughly with warm water and washing up liquid. Then check the horse thoroughly for injury, cleaning and dressing any cuts as necessary. Remove the studs and plug the stud holes, then trot the horse up to check for soundness, particularly if you know he hit a fence quite hard.

The legs must be treated to promote soundness and prevent filling — every competitor tends to have a favourite preparation which generally includes one or more of the following:

Tendon cooling lotion or gel rubbed briskly into the tendons. Check for contra-indications — some gels must not be used undiluted beneath bandages.

Ice-tight, Amoricaine paste or similar — clay-based mixtures which form a sticky paste. These are spread over the tendons, cannon bones and fetlock joints. They set dry and act as a cooling astringent.

Cold Animalintex or kaolin poultices can be safely used beneath bandages.

Ice packs — there are several ice pack preparations available, some of which are incorporated in their own special bandage.

Bandaging will help to prevent filling and promote efficient circulation within the lower limbs.

Once back at the stables the legs can be cold hosed if desired.

Back in the stable — further checks

The horse will be rugged up in accordance with weather conditions and can now be given a net of soaked hay. The early evening feed may consist of an easily digestible mash, possibly with milk powder or boiled linseed added. Electrolytes may also be added to the feed. The normal feed rations can be given later in the evening.

The horse must be checked for 'breaking out' (sweating). If this occurs, he must be towelled dry, then fitted with dry rugs and walked about.

At a three day event, it is especially important that all knocks and bumps receive attention to ensure that the horse is sound for the following day's veterinary inspection. The horse must then be allowed to rest in peace until late evening, when he can be led out to check for and relieve stiffness.

The following day

Walk the horse out very early in the morning to ascertain to what extent he has stiffened up. It is natural for the horse to appear stiff, but he should loosen off during a half hour walk out. A gentle hack out will also help loosen him. If the horse appears lame and you cannot deduce why, consult the vet.

(If back home after a lesser event, turn the horse out to grass for several hours to relax, roll and generally unwind. A short spell in the field works wonders for the horse's mentality, relaxes stiff muscles and removes filling from the limbs.)

Give slightly reduced short feed rations, ensuring the inclusion of electrolytes, and increase hay rations.

The final horse inspection

At a three day event there is a veterinary inspection in the morning of the final day. The horse must be well suppled up beforehand and immaculately turned out. Whilst waiting for the trot up, the horse should be kept walking around with a rug on. Double check for any stones in the feet.

Should the panel not be satisfied that a horse is sound enough to continue in the competition he may be held over for a second look. If, on the second trot up, the horse still does not look right he will fail the inspection — this is known as being 'spun'.

The showjumping phase

Generally the horses jump in reverse order, that is to say the leading riders jump last. After tacking up as appropriate, the horse is suppled up, spending a lot of time at walk, and encouraged to jump carefully and steadily in contrast to the previous day's style of jumping. Once the showjumping phase is over, horse and rider may hopefully be required for the prize-giving. There then follows the job of packing everything up to take home.

DRESSAGE

The governing body of international dressage is the Federation Equestre Internationale (FEI). Each nation has its own organization affiliated to the FEI. In Great Britain, the British Horse Society sets dressage tests of differing grades. The grades are Preliminary, Novice, Elementary, Medium, Advanced Medium and Advanced. Each grade sets clearly defined objectives regarding the horse's level of training and provides a means of assessing progress throughout the horse's career. Competitions may or may not be affiliated to the BHS. In affiliated competitions, points are awarded for the various placings. As the horse acquires an increasing number of points, so he moves up through the grades.

Horses will progress through the grades at a rate dependent upon several factors. For a dressage horse to be successful he must have as near perfect conformation as possible, combined with straight and impressive movement. He needs to have a strong back, quarters and joints. The hocks are particularly important as the hindquarters have to become progressively more engaged so that the horse's forehand becomes lighter as his level of training increases. Temperament is also important — the horse must be willingly submissive, accepting the aids without tension or resistance. To these factors can be added natural ability, and the skill and dedication of the rider/trainer.

Any horse or pony (there is no lower height restriction) can be registered with the BHS Dressage Group from the age of four years onwards.

Preparation

It is beyond the scope of this book to discuss the preparation of a horse for dressage in full — the work involved takes several years and requires expert tuition if high levels are to be attained. It is, however, relevant to state that attention must be paid to fitness. As no fast work is involved it is not necessary to have the horse eventing fit but, nonetheless, dressage does make physical demands of the horse — and these increase as the horse progresses and the tests become more difficult. In order to perform the movements well, and to avoid the possibility of physical strain, it is necessary for the horse to be made supple through progressive work. It is also essential that he is sufficiently fit and well to be 'thinking forward'.

Schooling at home is the foundation of the horse's training. Schooling sessions need to be of a duration and frequency to suit the individual horse. Many successful competitors supplement such schooling with other work, including moderate amounts of fast work and jumping. Performed correctly, such work helps stretch the horse's topline and encourages the development of impulsion. Hacking will provide variety, keeping the horse's interest and contributing towards fitness. Turning out for a few hours daily allows him to relax both mentally and physically — an important consideration for any competition horse, whatever his discipline.

SHOWJUMPING

The British Show Jumping Association (BSJA) is the governing body of showjumping in Great Britain. The BSJA lays down rules for many different types and levels of competition for both junior and senior riders. Competitions may be affiliated or unaffiliated to the BSJA. In affiliated competitions, horses and ponies are graded according to their monetary winnings, progressing up the scale as their winnings increase. All horses start as Grade C (ponies JD), becoming Grade B and A as winnings reach higher levels (ponies JC then JA). The grading limits are specified annually in the BSJA Rules and Year Book.

A showjumper needs to be athletic and bold, yet careful. Good conformation will maximize his chances of staying sound throughout his competitive career. In particular, the hindquarters must be strong to provide the power needed when jumping. The different conformational characteristics desirable in the competition horse have been discussed fully in another book in the series. *The Horse: Physiology.*

Preparation

The horse needs to undergo a basic fittening programme but, as he is working over shorter distances and at slower paces, he does not need to be as fit as the event horse. He does, however, need to be supple and balanced, and able to cope with short bursts of faster work in jump-offs.

Flatwork at home is essential to improve obedience, balance and suppleness. For a showjumper to be really successful, the flatwork must be of a high standard. Gymnastic jumping (gridwork) will teach the horse to be more athletic and can improve overall jumping technique. As with other types of competition horse, hacking aids fitness and provides variety, and time spent turned out aids mental and physical relaxation.

ENDURANCE RIDING

This sport is becoming increasingly popular, attracting riders of all ages and abilities. The introduction to endurance riding is generally through non-competitive pleasure rides which are sometimes sponsored to raise funds for charities. These rides are between 16 and 40 km (10 and 25 miles) with a minimum speed of 9 kph (5 mph).

As a rider becomes more enthusiastic, it is possible to progress onto more testing rides where, according to the level of competition, horse and rider have to cover a set distance in a specified time. Both horse and rider need to be fit in order to cope with variations in terrain, temperature and humidity.

Throughout the rides there are veterinary checkpoints at which the horse is examined for galls, cuts, sores, unsoundness and dehydration. His temperature, pulse and respiration rates are noted. The horse is only allowed to continue if the vet is completely satisfied that all is well.

The main governing bodies for endurance riding in Great Britain are the British Horse Society Endurance Riding Group (BHSERG) and the Endurance Horse and Pony Society (EHPS). Both bodies organize a programme of events.

BHSERG Rides

The competitions are split into the following categories:

Bronze Buckle Rides.

Silver Stirrup Rides.

Golden Stirrup Rides.

The Golden Horseshoe Ride.

Race Rides.

Bronze Buckle Rides

This category is further divided into two — Qualifiers and Finals. The Qualifiers are held over 32 km (20 miles) at a minimum speed of 10.4 kph (6.5 mph) and the finals are held over 48 km (30 miles) at a minimum speed of 11.2 kph (7 mph). Horses must be four years old at least. Any rider below the age of thirteen years must be accompanied by a mounted adult. During the veterinary inspections the horse's pulse rate is taken and, if it exceeds the specified rate (normally 64 beats per minute) the horse is eliminated.

Silver Stirrup Rides

These are also split into Qualifiers and Finals. The Qualifiers are ridden over 64 km (40 miles) at 11.2 kph (7 mph) and the Finals over 80 km (50 miles) at 12 kph (7.5 mph). Horses must be at least five years old and registered with the BHSERG. Young riders must be at least ten years old and accompanied by an adult. The minimum age to compete in the finals is eleven years; the rider may then be unaccompanied. All riders must belong to the BHSERG.

Golden Stirrup Rides

These fill the gap between the Silver Stirrup Finals and the Golden Horseshoe Rides. They are ridden over a distance of 96 km (40 miles) at a minimum speed of 12 kph (7.5 mph).

Horses must be at least six years old and riders must be at least twelve years old and BHSERG members.

Golden Horseshoe Qualifier

In order to compete at this level the horse and rider must have completed the bronze and silver series. This Qualifier is over 64 km (40 miles) at 12 kph (7.5 mph) and horses must be over six years old.

Golden Horseshoe Rides

Both horse and rider must successfully complete a Qualifier in the same season. The Golden Horseshoe Ride is over a distance of 160 km (100 miles) across Exmoor, to be completed in two days. Awards are presented in accordance with speeds achieved and veterinary penalties. Gold awards are given to horses and riders who finish with no penalties, having averaged 12.8 kph (8 mph) on each day. Silver and bronze awards are presented to other riders according to the penalties incurred and speeds achieved.

Race Rides

The competitor with the fastest total time (including time taken at compulsory halts), whose horse passes the final vetting, is deemed the winner. The distance covered varies and the minimum speed is 10.4 kph (6.5 mph).

The points system

Throughout the Bronze, Silver and Gold series, points are accumulated. One point is given for every mile completed in Bronze Buckle Qualifiers and Finals and Silver Stirrup Qualifiers, two points are given for each mile completed in the Silver Stirrup Finals and Golden Horseshoe Qualifiers, and three points are given for every mile in the Golden Horseshoe. At the end of the season, awards are presented based upon this points system.

EHPS Rides

The EHPS organizes Pleasure Rides, Competitive Trail Rides and Endurance Rides.

Pleasure Rides

These events are ideal for inexperienced riders and are run over distances of 32–40 km (20–25 miles) at speeds of 9.6–11.2 kph (6–7 mph). Horses must be at least five years old and must not be graded long distance horses.

Competitive Trail Rides

Competitive Trail Rides are run over distances of between 40 and 96 km (25 and 60 miles) depending upon the category. There are three categories: Novice, Open and Junior.

These rides are judged on the speed and condition of the horse throughout the ride. An optimum time is set and penalties are allocated if it is exceeded. Penalties are also given for speeds in excess of those needed to achieve the optimum time.

During the veterinary inspections, penalties are given for pulse and respiration rates which exceed those laid down. If either is excessively high, the horse will be eliminated. Injuries are penalised and lameness incurs elimination.

Endurance Rides

These are races — everyone starts together and the winner is the first combination to cross the finish line who successfully passes the vet's inspection. In the event of a tie, the winner will be the horse whose pulse and respiration are lowest after thirty minutes.

At the start of an endurance ride, each horse is checked and his pulse taken by the vet. Throughout the ride there are compulsory halts and spot checks. The first spot check may be after five miles — if the horse's pulse rate has risen to 64 or more the horse will be held until it is lowered. In some cases, the vet may eliminate the horse. The first halt is generally at the halfway mark and lasts for half an hour. Spot checks are carried out at specified points throughout the ride. It is sensible to walk the last mile before a check so that the horse's pulse and respiration can come down.

Horses for endurance riding

Endurance riding is one sport in which the majority of horses and ponies can happily take part at appropriate levels providing they are fit and sound. There are, however, some important points to consider when assessing suitability.

It is important that the horse will work in company or alone and not become distressed and badly behaved if held back from the others. A horse who is prone to misbehaving will tend to have a high heart rate, which could cause problems at the veterinary checks and even lead to his failing to start or being eliminated on the ride.

Good basic conformation and a free-flowing, straight action will help to ensure soundness. A long stride will cover the ground more economically than a shorter one.

Native breeds tend to be sensible and sound and are also hardy, sure-footed and safe. The Thoroughbred, however, is prone to an excitable nature, which can be a disadvantage for the reasons just given. Thoroughbred/Native crosses may well combine the sensible nature of the native with the staying power of the Thoroughbred.

Some cobby sorts may find working in hot weather distressing — a point to be borne in mind when planning the season's competitions. Arabs tend to cope with high temperatures and levels of humidity very well and, as the level of competition increases, the Arab comes into the limelight. This breed is renowned for soundness and stamina combined with giving a light and comfortable ride — qualities which make it ideal for long distance riding. Arab crossbreds are also very useful.

Preparation and training

Having decided to take part in a long distance ride you must choose a suitable event at which to start and plan a training programme accordingly.

The age and experience of both horse and rider will determine the level of competition — the most sensible plan would be to start with a pleasure ride of approximately 24 km (15 miles) and build up to a 32−40 km (20−25 mile) ride. About two weeks before the first competition try riding about 24km (15 miles) at approximately 10 kph (6 mph).

To take part in a 40 km (25 mile) ride the horse will need to be hunting fit — the fittening programme has already been discussed in full.

It will also be necessary to accustom the horse to different types of terrain, such as hills and moorland. Water crossings must be practised as should the opening and closing of gates — a procedure which, done quickly, can save a lot of time.

As we have seen, the optimum speed to be maintained will vary according to the level of competition. It is therefore necessary to practise attaining the required speed and keeping to it over a known distance. A car driven alongside is one method of gauging how fast a horse is travelling. Through practise it will also be possible to determine the horse's most economical gait; it is often less tiring and faster to maintain a rhythmic, flowing trot than a steady canter interspersed with walk. The speed at which you travel will be affected by the terrain and climatic conditions — factors which should be borne in mind both during training and competition.

Whilst training, practise reading a map and compass. Use them both in an area that you know well until you are confident that they will be of assistance to you in strange surroundings. Your map and compass can be carried conveniently in a clear plastic bib.

When fittening the long distance horse you should aim to produce a horse who finishes his ride happily in good, sound condition. This should also apply to the rider! A certain level of fitness will be achieved through the daily riding and stable work involved, but this may not be sufficient. Brisk walking, jogging, swimming and skipping help to increase heart and lung capacity. A supple, fit rider is far more use to a horse who begins to tire.

In the second season, it is usually easier to achieve fitness, having already got the horse fit in the previous year. Depending upon the success of the first year, you may aim to build up to 64—80 km (40—50 mile) rides in the second. Obviously, the horse will need to be fitter than previously.

As we have seen, horse and rider will be awarded gradings according to the number of penalties incurred for speed, pulse rate or injuries. It is necessary to achieve gradings as a qualification for higher competitions. The relevant rule books contain all of the necessary information regarding qualifications and gradings.

Equipment and clothing

When starting off in the sport at 32 km (20 mile) level there is no need to buy any sort of specialist tack. Normal, well-fitting tack and riding wear will suffice. Once the competitions are of 64 km (40 miles) duration or more, the choice of tack becomes more crucial. There are specialist long distance saddles available, custom-made with comfort of horse and rider as prime considerations. Some riders use a combination headcollar/bridle — for convenience the cheek pieces unclip, so removing the bit.

Headgear for the rider must be either the jockey skull cap BS 4472 or the riding hat BS 6473. For comfort, a lightweight crash cap or hat is best.

The rider may wear any type of footwear. Some people choose to wear trainers or walking boots if they intend to dismount and lead their horse. Trainers are permitted provided that caged safety stirrups are used.

It is wise to carry waterproof over-trousers and jacket rolled up in a saddle bag or pocket and to wear layers of cotton-mix clothing which may be discarded if necessary.

It is permissible to carry a whip provided that it does not exceed 76 cm (30 in) but spurs are not permitted.

The competition

Each competitor will receive notes giving information about the route, start time, time of veterinary inspection checkpoints and optimum time. It is necessary to calculate the speed at which each section is to be covered and how long it will take to reach each checkpoint. Once the exact start time is known, the time each checkpoint will be reached can be calculated. A record of these times must be kept and a copy given to the team of helpers. Depending upon the level of competition, there is usually a briefing at which the ride organizers explain the route and give out important information such as what to do and who to contact in case of emergency. It is useful for the helpers also to attend the briefing. Once the route is known it can be marked on the relevant ordnance survey map, again making sure that the team has a copy. The checkpoints may be visited if convenient — during the competition the team must be sure to arrive at each checkpoint before the rider.

The car will be required, packed with all the necessary equipment. This includes:

Full water containers — one with electrolytes already dissolved.
Buckets.
Spray bottles.
Sponges.
Sweat scrapers.
Anti-sweat sheets.
First aid kit for horse and rider.
Spare bridle, bit, numnahs, girths, girth sleeve.
Spare set of shoes.
Electrolyte powders.
Spare breeches, jacket, boots and gloves for the rider.
Energy foods and drinks for the rider.
Stethoscope for checking the pulse (horse's!).
Cooler box for ice packs.

The pre-ride veterinary inspection

You will be notified of the time of your pre-ride inspection. Plan to arrive at least one hour before this.

On arrival, collect your number from the secretary and find out if there have been any alterations to the route. Report to the veterinary steward five minutes before your setting time with the horse wearing a bridle only. Do not oil the hooves.

The vet will make a note of each horse's normal temperature, pulse and respiratory rates and these will be recorded as his base rates. Any changes are measured from the base rates. The horse is trotted up and any abnormalities of gait are noted. At subsequent vet checks any alterations from the norm will be classified as lameness. Old injury scars are also noted. All details are written down on the horse's own veterinary record card.

Vet gates

Depending upon the length of the ride there are a number of 'vet gates' to be passed through. There is a minimum of two gates on a ride. The rider must stop at these points and, within twenty minutes, present the horse to the vet so that he may check the pulse and respiratory rates.

The helper can listen to the heart rate through the stethoscope and, if it is below 64, the horse can be presented to the vet. If the vet records a heart rate of 64 or below the horse is then trotted for one minute exactly and the heart rate is taken again. Once again, it must be 64 or below. This is known as the Ridgway Trot or Cardiac Recovery Index. Once the horse has passed this and the vet is happy that the horse is sound and well, horse and rider can set off again. If a horse is presented *within* ten minutes of arrival and fails this test he may be re-presented. However, if a horse is presented ten minutes or more *after* arrival and fails, he is eliminated.

The sensible rider will try to approach the vet gates at a steady pace to ensure a low heart rate upon arrival. The sooner the horse can be safely presented to the vet, the sooner horse and rider can be on their way. At all checkpoints, the horse must be encouraged to drink and be sponged down. It is also important that the rider drinks plenty of fluids and eats energy-giving snacks.

The halfway halt

This is a compulsory halt with vetting taking place twenty minutes after the arrival of horse and rider. The vet will watch the horse come in and assess his general condition. The rider will dismount and allow the team to attend to the horse. The girth must be loosened — if wet with sweat, girth and numnah must be replaced. The horse can be encouraged to drink as much as possible; do not fuss over him with sponges etc. until he has quenched his thirst. He can then be well sponged to cool him. If the weather is very hot he may need to be sprayed with water and have ice packs held on the large superficial veins, such as those inside the hind legs. Water must be constantly available to him.

If necessary, electrolyte drinks may be given *in known solution*. While electrolytes can be very beneficial, an over-concentration (especially giving them undiluted) can exacerbate dehydration — and even cause death.

After twenty minutes, the vet will measure the pulse and respiratory rates and check for lameness, cuts, etc. Once all is deemed well, horse and rider may continue. However, if the pulse rate is above 64 or the horse appears dehydrated he will be eliminated.

Throughout the ride, the horse must be encouraged to drink at every opportunity to reduce the risk of dehydration.

The final vetting

This takes place thirty minutes after completion of the ride. The rider dismounts and the girth is loosened. The horse should be walked around to ensure he doesn't stiffen up and to help the dispersal of lactic acid. He must be allowed to drink freely and, after a few minutes, he can be completely untacked. He must be well sponged and any cuts washed and treated. The hooves also can be picked out and scrubbed.

If it is a cool day, cover the horse's loins and hindquarters with a suitable rug to keep him warm. He can be quietly led about to prevent him from stiffening up, and allowed to pick at some grass or hay.

The vet will measure the pulse rate first, and penalties will be awarded according to how far it is over the base rate. The respiratory rate is also assessed and if the horse is panting or his breathing is laboured he will be eliminated. Lameness incurs elimination and penalties may be awarded for lost shoes, saddle sores, galls and sore mouth. If the horse is eliminated for any reason, permission must be granted by the vet to travel the horse home.

In a world class FEI competition the final vetting takes place within 30 minutes of completion.

After-care of the horse

If the event is a long way from home, it is necessary to stable away. The night after the competition the horse should be allowed to rest and recover at his competition stable rather than be subjected to a long homeward journey. Obviously, you must consider the length of the journey, that of the ride completed and how tired the horse seems.

Once back in his stable, the care is very much the same as for the eventer or hunter:

1) Provide a good, deep bed, plenty of clean, fresh water and a full haynet.

2) Brush off and put on appropriate dry rugs. Check for cuts, etc. and treat accordingly. If the ground has been hard, apply cold poultices to the legs, held in place with stable bandages over gamgee.

3) After a couple of hours, give an easily digested mash with electrolytes added.

4) Later that evening check for 'breaking out' and change rugs if necessary. Give a more substantial feed.

5) Refill water buckets (one with plain water, one containing an electrolyte solution) replenish haynets and skip out.

The following morning:

1) Remove bandages, massage legs and check for heat and swelling.

2) Give easily digested feed with electrolytes added.

3) Walk out and check for lameness.

4) If possible, turn out for several hours.

5) If travelling home, walk out for half an hour to promote circulation and ease stiffness before loading. Remember to give an easily digested feed at least an hour and a half before travelling.

POINT-TO-POINTING

The point-to-point season starts in January and ends in May. When calculating a fitness programme for the point-to-point horse, it is necessary to take account of whether the horse is due to compete early in the season or is to start later on.

When selecting races, the going must be considered. Obviously, the weather greatly affects the ground conditions, but some courses have a natural tendency to be firm or soft and this may affect a horse's ability to gallop well.

Before a horse may compete in a point-to-point he must be qualified. This entails being 'regularly and fairly hunted', a description which is open to various interpretations but nowadays requires that the horse goes out hunting or cubbing at least seven times, commencing no earlier than 15th October. A certificate is then signed by the MFH and must be sent to Wetherby's for registration. With the exception of the Members' Race all horses must be registered in order to compete in a point-to-point.

Generally, point-to-point horses are hunted regularly before Christmas in order to qualify before the New Year. This allows time to get them racing fit by the start of the season. Even if there is no intention of racing in the early part of the season, it makes sense to qualify as early as possible since bad weather in January and February can lead to the cancellation of meets, which will disrupt the qualification process.

Often pointers will have a short break over Christmas to prevent them from souring. Horses known to take a long time to get fit may, however, remain in work. After Christmas, the fittening programme is geared towards achieving race fitness in time for the first planned meeting. At this point the horse will be hunting fit but nowhere near race fit — another four to six weeks fittening work will be needed, dependent on the horse's level of fitness. Although there is some variation, the majority of point-to-points are run over approximately 5 km (3 miles) and entail jumping some eighteen brush fences 1.3 m (4 ft 3 in) in height. To achieve success and minimize the chance of

injury, both horse and rider have to be fit enough to do this at
a racing gallop.

Fittening programme

Basically the pointer can follow a similar programme to the
event horse, with extra canter work. Long, slow canters will
develop stamina, fast work is kept to a minimum. The following
are examples of the type of programme followed to take a horse
from hunting fit to racing fit.

Example 1

Day One	$1\frac{1}{2}$ hours walk, trot and a steady canter over 1.5 km (1 mile).
Day Two	1 hour walk and trot.
Day Three	Walk, trot and steady canter over 3 km (2 miles).
Day Four	As day two.
Day Five	As day three.
Day Six	Steady canter for 1.5 km (1 mile), half an hour walk and trot, 1 km (5 furlong) gallop at 600 mpm. (Or a race).
Day Seven	Rest. (Especially if the horse is prone to tying-up, ensure that he is turned out or led out in hand.)

Example 2

Day One	$1\frac{1}{2}$ hours walk and trot.
Day Two	Steady warm-up to 3 km (2 mile) gallop at 500 mpm, followed by gradual winding down.
Day Three	As day one.
Day Four	As day two.
Day Five	As day one.
Day Six	As day two, including uphill sprint (but not to horse's limits) in last km (5 furlongs) of 3 km (2 mile) gallop. (Or a race).
Day Seven	Rest. (See note on rest day in first programme.)

As with all fitness programmes, each horse's individual requirements must be catered for and programmes adapted accordingly. However, the horse should never be galloped over the full race distance — this is tiring and may sour him. As fitness develops, it is beneficial to gradually increase the speed, but reduce the distance — a three-quarter speed gallop may be maintained over a maximum distance of 2.5 km. ($1\frac{1}{2}$ miles). Short, sharp bursts at *near* maximum speed act as a good pipe-opener for a horse known to be thick in his wind, but the fast work must never be overdone.

Schooling over fences

When out hunting, horses tend to be taught to jump carefully with a big steady, jump. In preparation for point-to-pointing, the horse needs to learn how to 'gallop on' over fences without being checked, maintaining a smooth rhythm. A novice horse can learn initially by taking a lead from an older, more experienced horse and then galloping on beside him over fences. It is important that the horse is confident jumping alongside others at racing speed before the first race.

Once the racing technique has been learnt thoroughly the fitness work can be interspersed with schooling to help keep the horse interested and supple.

Preparation for race day

Generally, pointers are shod with lightweight steel shoes — these are suitable for both daily work and racing. Some horses are plated — this involves putting on lightweight racing plates the day before a race and having normal shoes fitted afterwards. The disadvantages of this system include excessive wear and tear of the hoof, added expense and the extra time needed.

Shoes may have stud holes which are only ever in use with roadstuds fitted. No studs are permitted in a race because of the danger to fallen jockeys.

Racing tack

Races have varying requirements as to the minimum weight to be carried. A traditionally made steeplechase saddle of medium weight would be approximately 4.5−5.5 kg (10−12 lb). If the jockey and saddle fail to meet minimum race weight requirements, a weightcloth and lead will have to be worn beneath the saddle.

Stainless steel stirrup irons and buffalo or rawhide leathers should be used. In a race, always use leathers that have previously been stretched rather than new ones. The type of girths used is a matter of preference, but a pair of strong webbing or leather girths with elastic inserts allow for expansion of the ribcage whilst jumping and galloping. A surcingle or overgirth is always worn, and an Aintree breastplate will prevent the saddle from slipping backwards. Generally, a stainless steel snaffle bit is used with or without a cavesson noseband. Rubber-covered reins are essential − it is virtually impossible to hold a hard-pulling horse in anything else, especially if the horse is sweating and/or it is raining. An Irish martingale will help keep the reins together. In your own interest, and that of other race-riders, all tack must be double checked for safety every time it is used.

Pre-race preparation

The condition of the horse's shoes must be checked in time to allow new ones to be fitted if necessary.

The night before a race, the hay ration should be reduced to approximately 1.8 kg (4 lb). Bedding should be inedible to prevent the horse filling his digestive tract with bulk. On the morning of the race, the horse should not have hay unless he is racing very late in the day, in which case he may be allowed a small net first thing.

Some trainers remove the water buckets for a few hours prior to racing. If the horse is travelling in the lorry and then waiting for his race he should not be allowed to take a long drink, but his mouth can be washed out with a wet sponge to refresh him.

Horses are usually plaited up both for smartness and to avoid getting the reins or whip tangled in the mane. It is a good idea to use a shoelace to attach the headpiece of the bridle to the top plait — this will stop the bridle from being pulled off over the horse's head in the event of a fall. (It should be noted that trainers sometimes avoid plaiting certain horses because they associate the action with racing and become overexcited.) The tail may be plaited and, if desired, taped up out of the way; this is especially worthwhile if the going is heavy. Boots or bandages may be worn — bandages must be securely stitched or taped.

It is usual to arrive at the course at least an hour and a half before the start of the race. If the journey is long the horse may need to be walked in hand to loosen off, and the jockey will need to walk the course and weigh out. Forty-five minutes before the start of the race the horse is declared as a runner. He is then prepared and walked down to the paddock for the parade, some twenty minutes before the start of the race. The horse is led around for the parade wearing a paddock sheet over his saddle. An extra blanket will be needed if it is very cold, or a waterproof sheet if it is wet. Once the jockey has mounted, the girths are finally tightened before going down to the start (at which point, if requested, the starter's assistant will check the girths).

After-care of the horse

If the horse is placed in the first four, he must be taken to the winner's enclosure, where the jockey removes the saddle and weighs in. At this point the horse must not be allowed to get cold — suitable rugs will have to be on hand. An unplaced horse may return to the lorry immediately. In general, care after the race will be the same as for care after a cross-country round.

The following day

The horse should be trotted up to check for soundness and either walked out in hand or turned out.

If the horse does not pick up well after a race, he should have at least two weeks of gentle exercise to recover. If this occurs, examine the fitness programme and feed ratios, and consider having his blood tested.

Generally, soundness and weather permitting, horses will race six to eight times in a season. In between races the horse will require approximately $1\frac{1}{2}$ hours exercise daily. As discussed earlier, the amount and speed of work will vary according to the needs of each individual horse.

At the end of the season point-to-point horses are usually roughed off and turned away for the summer — again, trainers all have differing views as to the amount and type of break needed and the individual horse's requirements need to be considered.

POLO

The polo season starts at the end of April, finishing at the end of September. Each game consists of either four or six chukkas — a low goal game has four, a high goal game six. Each chukka lasts for seven minutes.

Each player will have a string of polo ponies — each pony generally plays one or two chukkas only per match, depending on fitness and ground conditions.

Preparation

The ponies are brought up at the end of February or beginning of March and walked out for approximately two weeks. Usually one pony is ridden and two led to facilitate exercising. It is alternated as to which pony is ridden. At the end of this initial walk period, trotting is introduced — the exercise sessions are of one and a half hours duration, of which half an hour is spent trotting.

Schooling is introduced around this time. During a match, polo ponies are required to work very hard for short spells, stopping and starting abruptly, accelerating and turning at speed. The pony must be taught the basics, usually as a four year old. Training will include stops, starts, acceleration, instant changes of leg and the turn on the haunches. All exercises should be taught initially at walk and gradually developed for use at the faster gaits. Once the basic movements are established the stick and ball can be introduced — when the pony is confident, other ponies and riders swinging sticks can be incorporated in the schooling sessions.

Approximately one month before the first match canter work is included — generally the ponies canter for twenty minutes a day as well as doing an hour's hacking. Occasionally a short burst at a half-speed gallop is used as a pipe-opener. The ideal work for a polo pony would be sprint-type bursts — something that is not always practical when exercising in threes.

As a five year old, a pony would play in minor games, building up to complete a full season as a six year old. It is important not to overplay a pony too soon as he may be soured and/or become unsound.

SHOWING

Preparation for the showing season tends to begin in early February following a winter break. Show horses usually remain stabled at night and well rugged throughout their break. Once back in work they may be clipped out to help establish the summer coat before the early shows. The horse needs to be well trimmed and kept warm with plenty of rugs. The exception is Mountain and Moorland ponies, who are shown untrimmed and unplaited and are not usually clipped.

All of the usual health checks must be carried out; teeth rasping, worming, inoculations and shoeing. Often, lightweight steel shoes or aluminium plates are used to encourage a light, 'floating' type of action. Stud holes should be fitted for outdoor shows where conditions may be slippery. If the horse has a tendency to stand 'toe-in', the toe clip of the fore shoe may be fitted slightly to the outside of centre. The toe clips on a horse who tends to stand 'toe-out' may be fitted to the inside of centre. Rolled toes are not usually used, as this could indicate faulty action or a foot problem.

Condition of animals

Show animals must look well covered and rounded, feel well and behave properly. This can be a difficult balance to achieve as most fattening foods provide energy which has a heating effect, particularly on ponies. Small ponies must be fed non-heating feedstuffs to ensure that they are safe for their riders and to prevent laminitis.

Many show animals carry too much fat — sometimes this is a deliberate attempt to disguise weak conformational points. It can be very detrimental to the horse's health as the excess fat will also lie around the heart and affect circulation. The extra weight puts additional strain on the heart, wind and limbs which, in the developing young horse, could have disastrous results. Soundness problems can also occur as the tendons, muscles and ligaments are overstressed; a show hunter needs to be able to gallop without strain on the heart and limbs.

Exercise

Show horses and ponies should have a variety of work, ranging from hacking to lungeing and schooling. Activities which may lead to injury and possible blemishes, such as hunting, are often avoided — although not by some of the most successful exhibitors! Nevertheless, sensible precautions must be taken: boots and/or bandages should be worn whilst working and kneeboots are a must when hacking out.

Some fat ponies are lunged wearing their rugs and hoods to encourage sweating as a means of weight loss — in such cases great care must be taken to ensure that the pony does not catch a chill.

Schooling at home should include teaching the horse to stand up properly and to be active and obedient when led up. At all times, good manners must be insisted upon.

Tack

Saddles

The saddle used must show off the horse's shoulder without being too uncomfortable for the rider or judge. Some showing saddles are cut too straight — a straight cut general purpose saddle may be more comfortable. A dressage saddle is suitable for hacks. A numnah is not normally worn unless the horse is prone to a cold back. Linen lined saddles are more comfortable for the horse but may not wear as well as a leather lined one. Hunters should wear leather girths; hacks and ponies, leather or white lampwick.

Bridles

Hunters, hacks and cobs are shown in double bridles or pelhams. All leatherwork is plain. Working hunters may wear a snaffle with or without a standing or running martingale. Whenever two reins are used the bridoon rein may be plaited to offer a better grip. The width of leather used should match the horse's build (hunters — medium width, hacks — fine, lightweight leather). The nosebands on bridles worn by hacks and ponies should have stitched patterns; the browbands may be coloured, either braided velvet or satin ribbon. However, coloured browbands are not worn by working hunter ponies.

Novice show ponies wear snaffle bridles; those in open classes wear double bridles. Mountain and Moorland ponies wear either a double or a pelham and should not have fancy stitched bridles.

In-hand classes

In-hand bridles should be made of the highest quality leather with finely stitched patterns in the noseband and browband. Brass linked, plaited leather or ribbon browbands are acceptable except for Mountain and Moorland ponies and hunters. Buckles should be neat and made of brass. If horses are shown in riding bridles, the buckles should be made of stainless steel and have plain browbands.

Regarding hunters, the tradition is as follows:

Brood mares are shown in either a double or snaffle bridle.

Foals wear either a foal slip or brass fitted headcollar with a white or leather lead rein.

Yearlings, two- and three-year-olds, if well behaved, do not have to wear a bit. If extra control is needed the bit, usually a mullen mouth snaffle, is buckled onto a brass mounted headcollar or bridle with a white browband. A long leather or white lead rein attaches to couplings on the bit.

Stallions usually wear a brass mounted stallion bridle with snaffle bit. A long lead rein is attached to couplings.

Turnout

All tack must be spotlessly clean. The horse must be bathed, well trimmed and socks whitened.

If plaiting before leaving home, the forelock and wither plait should be left. These will look tidier if done at the show.

The animal must be well rugged and bandaged in suitable clothing to keep him clean on the journey. Bandage to the end of the tail using two tail bandages.

Once at the show, warm up using a spare set of tack. Once warmed up, remove this tack and start to smarten up the animal. The socks may need to be re-washed and chalked. Thoroughly brush off surplus chalk. Groom thoroughly and wipe off dust with a stable rubber. Clean the eyes and nostrils then wipe the area with a small amount of baby oil to produce a sheen. Put quarter marks on with a comb, and dragon's teeth with a body brush.

Hooves should be oiled inside and out (after studs have been fitted if used). Whole-coloured horses with black feet should have hoof blacking applied while horses with white hooves and/or legs should have clear oil used. A dark shoe cream such as that from a ready-to-use applicator gives a strong, long-lasting colour.

If flies are problem use a suitable repellent — one that does not leave oily marks.

6

TRANSPORTING HORSES

Nowadays, competition horses are transported all over the world. As the way in which they are transported can affect their performance, the mode of transport needs to be considered carefully.

TRAILERS

The many manufacturers of trailers have sought to improve and update their designs to meet the demands of the ever-increasing number of horse owners wishing to transport their horses and ponies. Trailers are available to carry one, two or three horses or ponies and recently some form of living accommodation has been integrated into some of the designs.

Trailers provide an economical means of transport — anyone seventeen years of age or more with a full Group A licence may drive a vehicle towing a trailer, provided the gross (loaded) weight of vehicle and trailer does not exceed 3.5 tonnes. Once the age of eighteen has been reached, this weight limit is raised to 7.5 tonnes. At no time may a provisional licence holder drive a vehicle towing a trailer.

The normal permitted dimensions of a trailer are length 7 m, width 2.3 m — most horse trailers are well within these dimensions. The majority of trailers have two axles and four wheels in what is known as 'close-coupled' formation. These trailers are less likely to pitch and snake than the single axle, two wheeled type. (Pitch = seesaw action, snake = weaving action).

When considering towing a trailer you must take into account the power-to-weight ratio. The towing vehicle must weigh at least twice as much as the loaded trailer — most vehicle manufacturers offer advice regarding kerb weight, maximum recommended towing weight and recommended nose-weight of any trailer. The nose-weight is the force exerted by the trailer onto the towing attachment at the rear of the towing vehicle. Horse trailers are all designed to be within the safe limit. The kerb weight and engine power will determine the maximum towing weight. The permissible weight of a trailer depends upon its braking system. Trailers which do not have their own braking system must not exceed 750 kg (15 cwt) gross weight.

Braking systems

Unbraked trailers. These are dependent upon the braking capacity of the towing vehicle and their maximum gross weight must be displayed — this is usually painted to the left of the towing hitch. It is an offence to load a trailer beyond its maximum gross weight.

Braked trailers. These must have hydraulically clamped overrun couplings in order to comply with EC directives. Some of the older style trailers have spring-operated brakes which are being replaced in line with these directives. The hydraulically controlled piston gives a more progressive braking action: as a towing vehicle slows down the trailer attempts to overrun it, but pressure exerted via the coupling transfers to the linkage, causing the brakes to come into effect.

All trailers must have an effective parking brake.

Tyres

The tyres used on a trailer are regulated in the same way as tyres on a motor vehicle — under no circumstances may a mixture of cross-ply and radial be used on the same axle. Ideally, the trailer should have the same sort of tyres as the towing vehicle. In the event of the car having cross-ply tyres on the front and radial tyres on the back, the trailer may be fitted with either type.

Tyres must be checked regularly to ensure that:

1) They are inflated to the correct pressure.

2) The grooves of the tread pattern have a depth of at least 1 mm around the whole circumference and across at least three-quarters of the width. Any baldness (when the base of the groove pattern is no longer visible) is illegal.

3) There should be no deep cuts, lumps, bulges or excessive chafeing.

Lighting

The size and number of lights to be used on a trailer are stipulated by the Motor Vehicle Lighting Regulations. All trailers are required to have the following lights and reflectors:

At the rear:

Two red rear position lamps.

Two red reflectors — triangular reflectors must only ever be fitted to trailers.

Non-flashing brake lights.

At least one fog lamp — if only one is used it should be positioned on the righthand side.

Amber indicator lights, which should flash between 60 and 120 times per minute in unison with those of the towing vehicle.

A light to illuminate the rear number plate.

Trailers whose maximum gross weight is 3500 kg must have a red and yellow striped fluorescent marking.

At the sides:

Amber indicators showing to the rear.

Trailers whose overall length exceeds 5 m must have amber side reflectors fitted.

All lights and reflectors must be kept clean and in working order.

Other checks to be made include:

The connecting plug must be secured off the ground and covered to keep it clean and dry.

In the event of a fuse blowing, trace the fault before replacing the fuse with one of an identical capacity. Common electrical faults include loose bulbs and fuses, faulty connections, blown fuses and chafed wire insulation.

As the trailer draws its electrical power from the towing vehicle it is important that the battery is kept topped up with distilled water and the terminal connections are kept clear of corrosion, protected with a suitable grease.

HORSEBOXES

Any vehicle which is mechanically propelled and designed to carry goods or burden is classified as a 'goods vehicle'. This heading is then divided into a further two categories — heavy motor car and heavy goods vehicle.

Heavy motor car. Regulations regarding driver eligibility are as previously discussed (see Trailers). Horseboxes between the gross weights of 3.5 and 7.5 tonnes fall into this category.

Heavy goods vehicle. Any vehicle which has a gross weight in excess of 7.5 tonnes must be driven by someone holding a Heavy Goods Vehicle (HGV) licence and a normal full licence.

In order to take the HGV Test, a driver must hold the full Group A licence and be at least twenty-one years of age. Professional training is recommended in preparation for this test as advanced levels of driving proficiency and highway knowledge are demanded. A medical certificate will also be required before the HGV licence will be issued.

The Department of Transport stipulates the limits regulating driving hours, rest periods and the keeping of records under International, National and Domestic rules. Any driver of a lorry for private purposes, whether an HGV licence holder or not, is exempt from these rules. However, if any lorry is driven for hire or reward or in connection with trade or business, the driver becomes subject to these regulations.

Further details of these regulations are available in a booklet prepared by the Department of Transport.

Commercial vehicle regulations

Plating

Any vehicle with an unladen weight in excess of 1525 kg (30 cwt) must undergo an annual test known as plating. This test must be carried out at a Department of Transport Vehicle Testing Station and will include a check on all the important systems of the vehicle including the brakes, steering, chassis and electrical system.

If the vehicle passes the test, a plate is issued which shows the unladen and gross vehicle weights and the permitted axle loadings. The weight allowed over each axle plays an important role in maintaining the correct balance of the vehicle — there must never be too much weight over one axle, particularly the front axle when unladen. The plate is normally displayed inside the passenger door within the cab.

Commercial vehicles — those used in connection with a business or for hire or reward — are subject to spot checks by either an authorized examiner from the Ministry of Transport or by a uniformed police officer.

Operator's licence

Anyone using a lorry over 3.5 tonnes gross weight for hire or reward must hold an Operator's Licence. The purpose of the 'O' licence is to ensure the safe and proper use of goods vehicles and to protect the environment around operating centres. There are three types of licence:

Restricted licences are issued when the user wishes to carry their own goods in connection with their own business (known as 'own account'). Under no circumstances must a restricted licence holder transport other people's goods for hire or reward — anyone caught doing so is liable to lose the licence and be fined up to £500.

Standard National licences entitle the user to carry goods for other people for hire or reward anywhere in the United Kingdom.

Standard International licences entitle the user to transport other people's goods on international journeys including the United Kingdom.

Holders of the Standard National and International licences do not need to hold a restricted licence.

Certificate of professional competence

In order to apply for a standard licence, it is essential to hold the Certificate of Professional Competence. This exam is set by the Royal Society of Arts, who issue booklets explaining how to train for the exam and what is contained within the syllabus. It is possible to train for this exam either by attending a course run by the Road Haulage Association Training Department or through studying a correspondence course.

Other requirements which must be satisfied before a standard licence is issued include the financial standing and good repute of the applicant.

Tachographs

A tachograph is an instrument installed in the cab of a lorry to record the following:

Speed at which the lorry travelled.

Distance travelled.

Time spent driving.

Time spent resting.

Time off (spent resting) between working days.

Under United Kingdom and EC regulations all goods vehicles are required to use a tachograph, the exceptions being:

Any vehicle under 3.5 tonnes.

Specialized vehicles on national journeys.

Mobile exhibitions.

Vehicles used in connection with cultural events.

Equestrian leisure pursuits are counted as cultural events, therefore any horsebox used in a private capacity is exempt from having to use a tachograph. However, if horses are being transported for hire or reward in a vehicle of 3.5 tonnes or more, a tachograph must be installed.

The tachograph is installed and checked for accuracy (calibrated) at an approved vehicle manufacturer's or calibration centre. Once calibrated, the tachograph is sealed and a plaque giving the relevant information is affixed onto or near it. An approved chart is used in the tachograph onto which all details are recorded. The use of a tachograph is a complex subject — there are courses run by HGV training centres and a detailed booklet on the subject is available from the Department of Transport.

Road tax

Privately owned lorries used for leisure pursuits are liable to taxation at the same cost as a car. Any lorry used for hire or reward is subject to a higher road tax — the weight, its type and uses are all taken into account when the tax rate is calculated by the Excise Office.

Lighting requirements on horseboxes

The minimum obligatory lights and reflectors include:

To the front:

Two white position lights.

Two headlamps with dipping device.

Flashing amber indicators.

To the rear:

Two red position lights.

Two red non-flashing brake lights.

One illuminated rear number plate.

One red fog lamp.

Two red reflectors.

Flashing amber indicators.

To the side:

Amber reflex reflectors on all vehicles over 8 m.

Amber reflex reflectors on all vehicles over 6 m if first used on or before 1st April 1986.

Further regulations

The mechanical condition, construction and use of the vehicle are all covered by the *Motor Vehicles (Construction and Use) Regulations*. Other regulations which need to be considered include the *Transit of Horses Order 1951* and the *Transit of Animals Order 1931*. These regulations may be subject to change as new EC directives are drawn up.

Insurance

As with all motorized vehicles it is a legal requirement that they are properly insured — the minimum cover allowable is a 'third party' policy which will compensate for any damages affecting a third party. This policy does not cover the cost of repairs to the vehicle itself. For an additional premium, the vehicle may also be covered against fire and theft.

Since the cost of repairing a damaged horsebox can be so high, it is wisest to choose a 'fully comprehensive' policy which, in addition to the above-mentioned points, will also cover the cost of repairs. Dependent upon each individual insurance company's policy there will be exclusions of liability in the small print, which should be carefully checked.

Whenever transporting horses for hire or reward the 'Conditions of Carriage' must be established. The Road Haulage Association has compiled 'Conditions of Carriage' which are generally used by horse transporters. All clients and owners of horses must be aware of these conditions as they are taken into account when arranging a 'Goods in Transit' insurance policy. If extra cover is needed, the owner must make this known and the carrier must then arrange it.

Table 4. British Speed Limits for Trailers and Horseboxes

	Single Carriageway (unless a lower limit is specified)	Dual Carriageway	Motorway
Any vehicle towing a trailer	50 mph	50 mph	50 mph
Lorry not exceeding 7.5 tonnes	50 mph	60 mph	70 mph
Lorry exceeding 7.5 tonnes	40 mph	50 mph	60 mph

SPECIFICATIONS FOR HORSEBOXES AND TRAILERS

There are many excellent manufacturers of horseboxes and trailers, and much variation in materials used and overall design. The individual's choice of type, size and quality of vehicle chosen will largely be governed by funds available — you get what you pay for and where horseboxes are concerned, the sky is the limit! The following points are, however, worthy of consideration in all cases.

Structural features

Whichever material is used, the external bodywork must be safe, strong and visually pleasing. Weight is an important factor — wooden bodies can be heavy, and this may affect the way in which the vehicle handles as well as making the overall gross weight of the vehicle outside the minimum non-HGV limit. Glass-reinforced plastics are extremely popular and often used instead of wood or aluminium as they are tough, safe, hygienic and easy to maintain and repair.

Flooring

It is not ideal to leave the floorboards exposed as they are dangerously slippery when wet. Ribbed rubber matting provides a sturdy, non-slip flooring — ideally a few small holes should be drilled through this and through the wooden flooring to allow urine to drain away. (Any urine which seeps between the matting and the floorboards will rot the boards unless it can drain away.)

Another flooring material (known as Granilastic) is a rubber-based compound which is laid rather like cement in its wet form and then sets solidly. It has a roughened finish which helps to prevent slipping but can, however, make sweeping the floor rather difficult as the hay/muck particles get stuck to the surface. Granilastic is generally less susceptible to damage caused by horses wearing studs in transit although, if not laid properly, it can be prone to 'bubbling up'.

Ramps

The ramp must be of very strong construction, not too steep and ideally without a large step up at the top. Depending upon the positioning of the horses in the vehicle there may be more than one ramp — one at the rear and one or more on the side. The ramp must be non-slip — materials used include ribbed rubber, Granilastic or matting with wooden or metal slats. Horses wearing studs can damage the matting used on the ramp.

The ramp must be easily lowered or raised with correctly adjusted and lubricated springs or torsion bars.

Windows

Toughened glass must be used with non-injurous fastenings. Any glass below eye level, such as that found in the groom's door, should be protected with a wire mesh grille if it is in an area where the horses stand. This could prevent injury in the case of a horse 'pawing' at the floor or generally kicking around.

Ventilation cowl

In a lorry, ventilation is of paramount importance as it affects the horse's comfort and health. The ventilation cowl is usually positioned on the roof of the lorry and this must be borne in mind when driving beneath low branches. Some sophisticated lorries have air-conditioning. Lorries must *never* be draughty but must *always* be well ventilated.

Interior

The minimum permitted interior height is 2.2 m but this is often too low and will require considerable padding. It is not wise to travel large horses in a vehicle with such a low interior as they may feel claustrophobic and become panicky.

There must be no harmful projections such as catches and bolts — all fastenings must be very strong and kept well lubricated to ensure easy operation. Any breast or breeching straps or bars must be strong enough to withstand the full weight of a large horse.

Partitions

These must be very strong and, ideally, well padded. The partitions must be wide enough apart to ensure that the horse can spread his legs in order to find his balance. Partitions which extend right down to the floor offer protection against tread injuries as well as preventing a fallen horse from sliding under the partition and being trodden on by another horse.

If the partition is not solid to the ground, the lower section must at least be filled in with heavy duty rubber as a form of protection. Sniffer boards at head height help to prevent fighting whilst travelling.

Lighting

Power for lighting is usually drawn from the battery and is essential if planning to travel after dark. The more lighting that can be provided internally, the better. All light fittings should be at a safe height and protected by reinforced plastic. Obviously, wiring must be well concealed and out of reach of all horses.

A floodlight attached to the rear of the vehicle illuminating the ramp can be useful but must be positioned so that the horse is not dazzled as he is asked to walk up the ramp.

Storage

The manufacturers of lorries provide many different means of storing tack, equipment and feed. 'Hammock' type shelves running along the offside wall well above rump height are very useful. Some of the larger lorries, in which the horses travel standing diagonally, have feed bins built in just below chest level along the nearside wall beneath the windows. Roof racks can be provided for the carriage of hay bales. External storage areas can be built in within the bodywork, as can water carriers.

Living accommodation and tack area

The ideal arrangement is to have the living quarters of a lorry integral to the cab — this means that a passenger can, at any time of the journey, go and check the horses and communicate easily with the driver. There are many different designs of 'living' available, all with differing levels of facilities to suit every pocket. Some lorries have a separate tack area which provides further storage.

Position of horses

Most people have their own opinion as to which way a horse should face when travelling. Horsebox designers cater for all requirements and, provided the vehicle is safe and well ventilated and they have room to balance, the horses themselves generally don't mind whether they stand facing forwards, backwards or diagonally.

Maintenance

This is a vast topic, way beyond the scope of this book! The vehicle manufacturer will recommend when it will require servicing and how best to maintain it between services.

It is wise to remember that, if the vehicle is not in a roadworthy condition, the insurance is likely to be invalid.

Cleanliness and hygiene are extremely important — the inside of the vehicle must be regularly washed and disinfected, particularly if it is used to transport strange horses and ponies. The floors, partitions and walls should also be checked for damage or dangerous projections.

TRANSPORTING HORSES ABROAD

Transport abroad can involve travelling by sea and air as well as by road. Rail travel is less common for the normal movement of valuable animals — unfortunately many horses, ponies and donkeys destined for slaughter spend long, uncomfortable hours in cramped conditions aboard train carriages in some foreign countries.

Horses are usually transported abroad for competition purposes or to be sold. Because of the complexities of the rules and regulations imposed by each individual country, the movement of competition horses, racehorses and breeding stock is normally undertaken by professional horse transportation companies. These transport companies keep up to date with the many changes in laws and regulations, which may include periods of quarantine. They also attend to the required paperwork, which may include:

Health certificate. The test for this certificate is undertaken by a Ministry of Agriculture approved vet.

Passport. This must be up to date and show all of the important details including inoculation dates, etc.

Import licence. Requirements will differ from country to country.

Long journeys: preparation and precautions

Ensure that the vehicle is well serviced and that you have a supply of any small, important spare parts which may be difficult to obtain.

The transport company will advise you of any restrictions on medicines or feedstuffs that may apply in the country of your destination. If it is necessary to buy food there, it is worthwhile finding out what is available, buying some in advance and introducing it into the horse's diet before departure.

Make up sufficient feeds to last the whole journey, keeping each in a sealed plastic carrier bag for convenience. Depending upon the length of the journey and how the horse travels, all short feed should be reduced two to five days before departure. All feeds given should be low in carbohydrate and easily digested to reduce the risk of azoturia or colic as a result of long periods of enforced inactivity. However, keep to the normal hay rations, and be sure to offer water frequently to prevent dehydration.

Always carry a well stocked first aid kit including a short-acting painkiller which can be administered in the event of the horse suffering from colic whilst on the journey, for example on a ferry, when it might not be possible to get a vet to look at the horse for several hours.

If the destination is known to be hot and/or humid, introduce electrolytes into the diet at home to get the horse used to the taste.

Exercise the horse for at least one and a half hours before loading up, even if this means riding in the very early hours of the morning. During the journey (once off the ferry) try to lead out in hand or — if possible and safe — lunge the horse.

If held up on the journey, for example as a result of bad weather, cut back the short feed further. Extra hay may be fed to reduce boredom, maintain condition and keep the digestive system working. Do not neglect to give water.

Upon arrival, start gradually to build up the short feed so that the horse is on his normal working ration before the competition starts.

Prepare the horse for the homeward journey as for the outward one, by reducing carbohydrates and feeding succulents and hay.

Probiotics, feed supplements which enhance the balance of gut flora, are sometimes used to maintain optimum levels and to promote normal gut function. It is recommended, however, that these should not be given without first seeking veterinary advice.

Travelling by air

The transport company liaises with the airport authority to organize the actual loading of the horses — this job is always undertaken by skilled handlers employed to perform that specific task. The groom or owner should be present to stand with and reassure the horse during time spent waiting. The excitement of the noise and activity may frighten the horse, who may need distracting with a supply of sliced apples or carrots. The horse should wear a bridle for extra control and the appropriate clothing for protection and warmth. This clothing should be checked during the journey — rugs must be of a design that is easy to adjust, as space for manoeuvre is limited. Once the aeroplane is airborne most horses tend to relax and travel well. Note that it is not normally advisable to tranquillize horses travelling by air, as they need to be able to balance themselves properly.

Travelling by sea

The horses travel in the lorry within the hold of the ship. Ideally, the ramp should be lowered or at least partially opened to help the through-flow of air. The horses must not be left unattended — they will need water offered frequently and a regular check on warmth, with rugs adjusted as necessary.

Seasickness can affect horses very badly, with the effects lasting several days. Therefore, whenever possible, rough crossings should be avoided.

Having arrived at your destination there may be delays in getting through Customs — allow extra time for this.

Once you have arrived in the country of your destination, a phrase book and good map will come in useful. Once on your way, remember to drive on the appropriate side of the road!

7

PROBLEMS AFFECTING THE COMPETITION HORSE

In this chapter we shall consider how to detect and deal with various problems to which the competition horse is particularly susceptible. It should be noted, however, that prevention or avoidance of these problems is vastly preferable to cure — failing that, vigilance and early detection of warning signs may minimize the extent of the problem and maximize the chances of early and complete recovery.

STRESS

Stress may be described as a pressure or tension which places a demand upon both physical and mental energies. Provided that the level of stress is increased gradually, the body is able to adapt. Each time something stressful occurs the body will respond in such a way that next time the same or a similar challenge is met the body is better able to tolerate it. Such adaptive responses are an essential part of the fittening process.

A stressful situation has an effect upon the sympathetic nervous system which, when activated, prepares the body for flight. A neurotransmitter substance, noradrenalin, is released from nerve endings in response to an impulse passing along a nerve fibre of the sympathetic system. Noradrenalin causes the lungs, heart, spleen and sweat glands to react in preparation for flight. In the lungs, the airways become more dilated, allowing increased inspiration of oxygen. The heart rate is increased, improving the supply of blood to the muscles. Noradrenalin causes the spleen, which acts as a reservoir of red blood cells, to contract, releasing more red blood cells into the circulatory system, and sweating is initiated, helping to control body temperature.

Nerve fibres from the sympathetic system extend to the adrenal glands which lie in front of the kidneys. When activated, the adrenal glands release the hormone adrenalin which causes the release of glucose from the liver and free fatty acids from stores within the body, to further improve energy supply. The amount of adrenalin produced is affected by the intensity of the exercise, for example the degree of increase is greater when racing than when taking part in a long distance ride.

In the wild, survival is largely dependent upon the instinct of fright-flight-fight, a reaction which is clearly displayed in the domesticated horse in stressful situations. The stress reactions can be triggered off by a number of factors including:

Fear

Handling and weaning of youngstock.

Castration.

Breaking-in.

The progressively increasing workload of the fittening process.

Transportation.

Competing — performing in the competition atmosphere surrounded by strange horses, crowds etc.

The anticipation of competing, hunting etc.

The stress threshold will vary from one horse to another, depending upon his temperament and the competence of the handler/trainer. The competition horse is, however, under a constant level of additional stress and may thus be especially sensitive to changes. Too much stress will lead to physical and/ or mental *distress*. Depending upon the nature of the stress factors, this may be exhibited as one or more of the following signs:

Heat, pain and swelling — injury may occur.

Signs of ill health — including abnormal behaviour such as stable vices, and weight loss. Some horses go off their feed when fit and, if over-competed, become 'sour'.

Reactivation of a latent virus. Stress causes the adrenal gland to secrete cortisol, which is the body's anti-inflammatory agent. High levels of cortisol reduce the immune defences, allowing recrudescence of latent infections. There is also increased susceptibility to both viral and bacterial challenge, for example 'opportunist bacteria', normally found in horse's nasal cavities, may cause disease if the immune system is compromised.

Shaking. Electrolyte imbalances lead to problems with the conduction of impulses along nerves, and with contraction of muscles. Fatigued muscles have reduced co-ordination of contraction, and this may be evidenced by shaking.

'Thumps' — synchronous diaphragmatic flutter may occur in an exhausted horse suffering from an electrolyte imbalance. The thorax contracts in synchrony with the heartbeat. This condition is very serious, requiring immediate veterinary attention. It is dealt with in more detail in the next section — Dehydration.

Avoiding overstressing the competition horse

Much can be achieved by careful planning and common sense. Most importantly, ensure that the horse is properly prepared —

mentally and physically — for the level at which he is required to compete. Other than this:

1) Travel with care — before a long journey reduce energy feeds and give an easily digestible feed to avoid impaction and dietary disturbances. Ensure good travelling conditions; adequate ventilation with the horse rugged and bandaged suitably.

2) When fittening, assess each horse individually and adjust the work programme accordingly.

3) Warm up properly whether at home or at a competition.

4) In between classes use rest breaks sensibly, keeping the horse warm or cool depending on the weather conditions.

5) When away at a competition, try to keep to a stable routine as close as possible to that kept at home. This will help to make the horse feel secure.

6) Keep to the same feed rations at a competition. If permitted, pack enough hay and short feed to last the duration of the stay, particularly if competing abroad.

7) Whilst at the competition, allow the horse time to graze in hand and relax. At home, allow all competition horses some time to rest and unwind in the field every day. At the end of the season, such horses should have a complete break.

8) The day after strenuous activity, check the horse very thoroughly for signs of injury. Turn out or lead out to ease stiffness.

9) After a hard performance, adapt feeds to promote a speedy recovery. For example, add electrolytes and a nutritious feedstuff such as milk pellets, boiled barley or linseed. The first feed given after hard work should be easily digestible and palatable, with a more 'serious' feed being given later in the evening.

DEHYDRATION

Any form of muscular activity generates heat. To maintain a healthy temperature this heat must be dispersed. Heat loss is achieved through the skin by sweating and through the lungs (expiration).

The skin. Heat generated within the muscles is taken in the blood, via the circulatory system, to the surface of the skin. Here, the superficial blood vessels dilate, allowing more blood to circulate close to the surface of the skin, thus facilitating more efficient cooling by radiation.

Sweating. Sweat is derived from blood plasma (extra-cellular fluid) and from within the various cells of the body (intra-cellular fluid). It is excreted into the environment via the sweat glands in the surface of the skin. As the sweat evaporates so heat is lost — this is a very efficient form of heat loss providing the air temperature and humidity are low. Sweating is even more effective when there is a breeze to speed up evaporation.

Sweating ceases to be efficient in very hot and humid conditions. The air will already have a high moisture content, which reduces evaporation. This is an extremely important factor to consider with any competition horse.

The lungs. Expired air is very warm and has a high moisture content. Once the skin cooling system has become ineffective a horse will begin to pant — this generally occurs once the horse is seriously overheated.

Causes

Dehydration is a condition resulting from the loss of fluids and electrolytes from the horse's body. Generally this condition occurs as a result of excessive sweating by a horse who does not receive enough to drink. Around 60 per cent of the bodyweight is made up of water. A loss of up to 5 per cent of body fluids will result in moderate dehydration, 8 per cent loss will result in illness and anything above a 10 per cent fluid loss constitutes serious dehydration (usually associated with heatstroke).

Moderate to heavy sweating can result in approximately 5 litres (9 pints) of sweat being lost each hour. A loss of 3 litres (5 pints) will result in a state of dehydration. Even in cool weather a horse may sweat between 6 and 8 litres (10–14 pints) an hour if working at a steady canter. This will not cause problems if the humidity is low and the horse is given plenty to drink. The exact amount of water needed daily will depend upon the age, size and temperament of the horse combined with his work, diet and environmental conditions. The potential variation is substantial — somewhere between 18 and 76 litres (4–17 gallons). (NB provided the endurance horse is kept moving after a drink it is quite safe to allow him to quench his thirst during a ride as the movement helps to warm the water. The event horse should also be allowed a small drink before the cross-country phase if he wants it. Recent studies have disproved the traditional view that this is harmful.)

Effects

Normal metabolism and cellular functions can only continue in the presence of the correct balance of fluids and electrolytes. Electrolytes are ions — substances which carry either a positive or negative electrical charge. Those most important to equine metabolism are sodium chloride (common salt), potassium, calcium, magnesium, phosphorus and the trace elements iron, copper, zinc, cobalt, selenium, sulphur and iodine. These are all lost through sweating — each litre of sweat lost may contain 7.5 – 10.5 g of sodium chloride and 1.5–3.5 g potassium along with various levels of the other elements. Normally, the fluid/electrolyte balance within the body is maintained by the kidneys. When significant quantities are lost through sweating, however, they can only be replaced through eating and drinking.

Physiological effects of fluid and electrolyte loss

As fluid is drawn out of the blood vessels to form sweat, the blood volume becomes reduced — the blood becomes more concentrated and has a thicker consistency. Because of the decrease in blood volume there is less sweating, therefore the body temperature increases. The effects of overheating will be discussed more fully further on (Heatstroke). However, the oxygen-carrying capacity of the blood is reduced, leaving muscles short of oxygen. Since another source of energy is required, the muscles begin to respire anaerobically, resulting in the release of lactic acid. This lactic acid may build up, particularly in the large muscle area of the hindquarters, and lead to muscle fatigue.

Once the skin cooling system has ceased to work, the horse may begin to pant heavily to try and lose heat via the lungs. In extreme cases, a condition known as synchronous diaphragmatic flutter ('the thumps') may occur. The diaphragm beats in rhythm with the heart, and this may be seen as a movement in the flank which is not related to normal respiratory movement. If the condition is serious enough, the movement may also be heard as a thumping sound. The exact cause is not known but, if a horse is seen to be suffering from the condition, a serious electrolyte imbalance is indicated. It is most often seen in endurance horses competing in very hot climates, and is treated by correcting the fluid and electrolyte imbalance.

Signs

In the early stages of dehydration, the horse becomes dull and lethargic. The pulse and respiratory rates will be high and will take a long time to return to normal.

As sweating stops, the temperature rises and the condition worsens. The coat will be covered in thick, patchy sweat and the horse may pant. The eyes may sink back into the sockets and the mucous membranes become reddened. Gut sounds are reduced. The horse may become disorientated and, in severe cases, develop colic and go down.

When diagnosing dehydration, there are three simple tests

which may be done. These are the 'pinch' test, the 'capillary refill' test and the jugular refill test.

The pinch test. Dehydration causes a loss of skin elasticity — normally a pinch of skin from the neck would recoil to its normal position immediately. If the skin takes longer than two seconds to recoil, the horse is dehydrated. The longer it takes to recoil, the more dehydrated the horse.

The capillary refill test. Press the horse's gum hard with one finger. This will leave a white mark which should immediately return to pink. If this takes two seconds or more, it indicates that the blood is too thick to circulate easily through the capillary network, therefore the horse is suffering from dehydration (or shock).

The jugular refill test. Run the thumb or forefingers down the jugular groove with enough pressure to squeeze the blood from the vein. Once empty, feel with the fingers as the collapsed vein becomes distended and refills. Normally it will refill in two seconds — a longer time can be considered a warning sign.

Table 5 gives guidelines for normal and abnormal responses when checking the horse.

Treatment

In mild cases, the horse must be encouraged to drink approximately 5 litres (1 gallon) of water every fifteen minutes. If the horse is accustomed to it, he may be offered an electrolyte solution. Electrolyte preparations are available widely and may be administered in the water or feed or given neat through a plastic syringe in the corner of the mouth. (Electrolytes must only be given neat if the horse's stomach contains plenty of water. Neat electrolytes in an empty stomach will draw water from the blood vessels to absorb them.) The electrolyte solution in drinking water must not be too strong as that,

Table 5. Guidelines for Performing the Vet Check on your Horse

Parameter	Green	Yellow	Red
Eyes	bright, clear	glassy	fixed stare, sunken eyeball
Mucous Membranes	pink, moist	pale, tacky	dry, purple, blue
Capillary Refill	0−1 seconds	2−3 seconds	4+ seconds
Jugular Refill	1−2 seconds	2−3 seconds	4+ seconds
Skin Pinch	0−1.5 seconds	2−3 seconds	4+ seconds
Heart Rate (after strenuous exercise)	<68 in 10 minutes	68 in 10−30 minutes	>68 in 30 minutes
Gut Sounds	normal	reduced/increased	absent
Respiratory Rate	relaxed/regular	panting/inversion	laboured/abnormal
Joints/legs	no heat or swelling	heat/swelling	heat/swelling/pain
Wounds/Saddle/Girth	no visible marks	heat/swelling/tender	pain/raw/bleeding
Muscles/Back	relaxed	tight, tender	very tight/pain
Anal Tone	tight	slightly loose	anus/penis relaxed
Rectal Temperature	<38.6°C pre-ride <39.6°C during ride	39.5°−40.5°C during ride	>40.5°C
Impulsion	free, willing	stumble/short stride	stiffness
Attitude	bright/eats/drinks	depressed/lethargic	dull, not interested; absence of thirst, appetite, urination or defecation
Gait	no abnormality	slight gait change	consistent gait change/non-weight bearing

Green Healthy responses
Yellow Warning signs − consult vet
Red Danger signs − veterinary attention urgently needed

too, will have an adverse osmotic effect, causing fluid to be drawn out of the blood supply to the gut and exacerbating the dehydration.

It is not possible to replace all of the elements lost through sweat in an electrolyte solution, as the water would be too salty to drink. However, electrolytes can be added to the feed for several days before and after a strenuous event to compensate for losses. Electrolyte preparations should contain four times more sodium than potassium as this is in keeping with the ratio of sodium and potassium losses. Some preparations contain glucose, dextrose or citrate to aid the absorption of the electrolytes.

The horse should also be sponged to cool him — cold water may be used on the large muscle masses provided that the horse is kept walking to prevent cramp-like conditions such as azoturia.

In normal weather conditions, cold water assists cooling as the water evaporates from the skin. The girth and saddle area can be sponged with methylated spirit, which evaporates quickly, leaving the area fresh and cool. In extreme heat and humidity ice packs on the top of the head, down the neck and on the insides of the hind legs will help cool the horse quickly, but he *must* be kept walking. Alternatively, copious amounts of cold water can be applied to these specific sites, being quickly scraped off to aid cooling.

The nostrils, eyes and dock must be sponged with fresh water. If the horse is severely dehydrated, veterinary assistance must be sought. Offer water constantly until the thirst is quenched.

Prevention

Dehydration is, obviously, a condition better prevented than cured. The following preventative measures should be borne in mind:

During the training of the long distance horse, teach him to drink at every opportunity, from clean streams and pools. Note that, while many endurance rides take place in areas where the natural water supply is cleaner than average, care should be taken to ensure a shallow, safe approach, a stony/gravelly bed and that the supply is clear and unpolluted.

(Some horses refuse to drink from such sources, and it should be noted that these rarely prove suitable for top level endurance riding.)

Accustom the horse to the taste of electrolytes in water, so that he will happily drink the solution at a competition.

Offer water frequently throughout a competition — every two hours at the minimum. The horse must be kept 'topped up' to avoid dehydration.

Before a competition, allow free access to fresh, clean water. Some trainers advocate that the event horse should have water removed for one hour prior to going across country but if he has had free access to water all day he is, in any case, unlikely to take a long drink.

During a long distance ride sponge the horse frequently. A sponge attached to the saddle on a long piece of string can be lowered into a stream or puddle and used to sponge down without having to dismount.

Be aware that, in hotter, humid weather, the risk of over-heating increases dramatically, so the speed at which a ride is completed may have to be reduced.

HEATSTROKE

A horse who is dehydrated in hot weather will also be susceptible to heatstroke. This is a potentially fatal condition from which any horse competing or exerting himself in unusually hot conditions is at risk. As previously discussed, energy production within the cells causes heat to be generated. The more strenuous the activity, the greater the amount of heat produced. This build-up of heat will be even greater in hot weather conditions.

The normal rectal temperature of a horse is 38 °C (100.5 °F) but the horse's actual core temperature (that of the internal tissues), will be approximately 1.2 °C (2.8 °F) higher. After activity, the temperature may rise to 39—39.4 °C (102—103 °F), which is not a cause for concern provided that the temperature does not remain static or increase further, or that the weather is not very hot and humid. Temperatures of 40 °C (104 °F) and above, however, indicate a critical level. If a temperature of 41 °C (105.8 °F) were maintained for any great length of time, the horse's life would be endangered. Temperatures as high as 42 °C (108 °F) and over are only seen in seriously ill horses. Tissue proteins actually break down in response to these high temperatures and death generally occurs.

If the body's cooling systems fail to lower the temperature to a safe level quickly, the horse will suffer from heatstroke. Heatstroke usually affects dehydrated horses in the latter sections of long distance rides or the cross-country phase of a horse trial in hot, humid conditions. A horse kept in a hot, ill-ventilated stable for many hours may also be affected. The state of dehydration causes a fall in blood volume which adversely affects cooling — sweating is greatly reduced. The core temperature increases — the rectal temperature will be high, 41.5—43.3 °C (106—110 °F). The horse will show signs of depression and weakness, accompanied by a high pulse and respiratory rate. The skin will feel hot and dry, and the horse may stagger about before going down. In very serious cases he may go into a coma before death occurs.

Heatstroke must be treated quickly under the advice of the vet. Before the vet reaches the horse try to move him into the shade, preferably in a breeze — fans can be used, if available. Hose or sponge down constantly with cold water, paying particular attention to the poll and the length of the spine. Avoid the use of icy water on the large muscle masses of the hindquarters. However, ice packs may be held over the large blood vessels on the inside of the hindquarters to cool the blood as it passes near to the surface of the skin. The vet will administer fluids intravenously to increase the blood volume.

TENDON INJURY

The tendons of the lower limb are under varying degrees of pressure depending upon whether the horse is simply walking around a field or competing. Whatever work the horse is doing the tendons are constantly changing — the old, worn fibres being replaced with new, young ones. Tendons are made up of bundles of collagen fibres which are arranged longitudinally and interspersed with collagen-producing cells known as fibroblasts.

Collagen is an inelastic fibrous protein which makes up the bulk of all skin, connective tissue, bone, cartilage and tendons. The type of collagen of which tendons are formed has a crimped structure which, if stretched, pulls straight then recoils, so helping to absorb and reduce stress and strain. As the collagen fibres become older and worn they lose their crimped effect, which results in a loss of elasticity.

The rate at which new collagen fibres replace old is dependent upon the adequate flow of blood bringing nutrients and oxygen to the area, and also correct pH levels. Blood circulation is increased and improved by regular exercise, therefore the collagen fibres are replaced more quickly, resulting in stronger tendons. The horse in less demanding work will not have such strong tendons and should never be overexerted suddenly. Repeated loading of a tendon tends to stabilize its mechanical response, making it both more elastic and stiffer. In this state, it is less susceptible to damage. This is why it is so important to warm up the horse gradually at the beginning of exercise.

Furthermore, a workout will cause some micro-damage to fibres within the tendons (and also, the ligaments). This is normally repaired between workouts, resulting in increased collagen content, increased cross-linking between fibres, and stronger insertions onto the bones. The result is stronger tendons (and ligaments) but, because these tissues react slower than any other musculoskeletal tissue, the process is very gradual (over a period of months). This inevitably limits the rate of the conditioning process.

Under normal healthy conditions the collagen in tendons should be renewed approximately every six months. However, interference with the oxygen supply, perhaps as a result of injury which impairs circulation, or insufficient recovery time between hard workouts, may lead to degenerative changes within the tendon, which will further complicate the healing process.

Signs

Early signs include localized heat and swelling — although the horse may not be lame initially. With more serious tendon strain there will be a greater degree of inflammation accompanied by severe lameness.

Causes

Muscle fatigue

Fatigue may result from bad going or overexertion of an unfit horse. Once the parent muscle becomes fatigued it becomes less co-ordinated, placing extra strain on the tendon which may then be overstretched.

Conformation faults

Various conformation faults may cause or contribute to injury:

1) Long cannon bones will have longer tendons which are more susceptible to strain than shorter tendons.

2) Limbs which are too small in relation to the size of the body may not be strong enough to support it properly.

3) An excessively sloping pastern/foot axis which exerts too much pressure on the tendons.

4) Mechanical injury may result from the horse striking into himself whilst jumping or galloping. Such injury may also be the result of misfortune, for example, putting a foot down a rabbit hole.

5) Degenerative injury. Poor circulation, and therefore poor oxygen supply, may be a result of faulty foot conformation. In such cases the collagen fibres are not replaced regularly.

As previously described the existing collagen loses its elasticity and is unable to withstand any level of stress. If subjected to regular stress, warning signs of heat and swelling may appear.

6) Contracted tendons. As a result of contraction of the digital flexor tendons the heel may be raised and the fetlock joint straightened. In severe cases the front of the fetlock joint may even touch the ground. This condition, sometimes referred to as 'knocking over', may be present at birth, or it may develop suddenly in youngsters as a result of tendon injury, infection or dietary deficiency.

Effects

Depending upon the nature and extent of the injury, the tendon fibres are torn or stretched. This may lead to haemorrhaging within the tendon, which stimulates other cell-bearing fluids to enter the injured site. These fluids seep through from adjacent tissues in order to clear away debris such as dead tissue and to fight against infection of the damaged area.

As a result of cells dying, toxic substances are formed. These irritate the surrounding tissue and this further stimulates the flow of blood to the area leading to inflammation (tendonitis). Where inflammation occurs beneath an annular ligament, extreme pressure is exerted on the inflamed area. This usually reduces circulatory flow, which can then lead to tissue death and bowed tendons ('low bow').

After an injury, the limb is generally naturally immobilized (the horse is reluctant to move) — this is a result of the pain and swelling. Further immobilization is enforced as the horse has to rest. This lack of movement leads to impaired circulation, as venous return is dependent upon muscle contraction. As a result of this the area becomes engorged with blood, fluids and cells, which solidify to form a haematoma.

In areas of intense inflammation, especially where a haematoma has formed, there is a danger of adhesions forming as a result of the loss of movement. Adhesions are areas where the healing tissues become stuck to over- and underlying tissues, which further limits movement. If adhesions are stretched, they break down and cause damage to adjacent areas.

In association with tendon fibre damage or as a reaction to an injury or blow, the tendon sheath may become inflamed. This is known as tenosynovitis.

The healing process

A few days after injury, new blood vessels begin to permeate the injured area, pushing their way through the engorged and swollen tissues. These blood vessels carry building cells for repair to the site, and also remove damaged tissue. The repair cells lay down collagen fibres to form a scar — sometimes referred to as granulation tissue. The repair collagen is not arranged longitudinally, but is placed in random fashion, an arrangement which has less tensile strength and therefore reduces the strength of the tendon. Eventually the fibres realign and are replaced, although the collagen with which they are replaced is of a weaker type. After a year or so this may again be replaced, this time with a stronger type of collagen.

Whenever dealing with tendon injuries it is necessary to bear in mind the time taken before the tendons are remodelled — in the year following injury the tendons will not be at full strength.

Treatment

The exact treatment given immediately will depend upon the nature of the injury. If the horse has struck into himself there will be an open wound to deal with. Any bleeding must be stopped and the wound thoroughly cleaned.

Although inflammation heralds the healing process the priority, for the reasons described above, is to immediately control and reduce it. Box rest will be essential in severe cases, to prevent the horse from using the limb and causing further damage.

Following the reduction of inflammation, surgical shoes may have to be fitted, for example raised heels to reduce pressure on damaged tendons.

The vet may recommend that an accurate diagnosis to determine the severity of the injury be obtained through the use of ultrasound scanning equipment.

It is thought that controlled passive motion with slight tension on the injured tendon in the acute repair stage (granulation tissue deposition) helps with orientation of the fibrils and reduces adhesion formation. However, finding a balance between mild tension to promote repair and more severe tension which compromises healing, remains a problem.

THERAPIES TO REDUCE INFLAMMATION

As we have seen, inflammation is part and parcel of most tendon injuries, but it may also occur in different parts of the body, for a variety of reasons. There are many treatments designed to reduce inflammation, some traditional and some 'high tech' and it is to the advantage of all who deal with competition horses to know something of them.

Basic methods of controlling inflammation include:

Cold therapy.

Hydrotherapy.

Heat therapy.

Therapy machines which facilitate treatments such as magnetic field therapy, ultrasound, laser, Electrovet, Ionicare and faradic therapy.

Massage.

Support.

Anti-inflammatory drugs.

Cold therapy/hydrotherapy

Cold treatments can be used immediately after injury. The effects on the injured tissues include:

Vasoconstriction. The blood vessels tighten and so blood flow is reduced. This helps to control the formation of haematomas (blood-filled swelling) and oedema (fluid accumulation in tissues) beneath the skin. Vasoconstriction also assists in stopping bleeding in an open wound.

Vasodilation. This has been found to occur in the deep tissues of the area in response to the intense cold when ice treatments are in place for ten minutes or more. Vasodilation follows vasoconstriction, which has the effect of increasing circulatory flow through the area.

Analgesia. The immediate, temporary, analgesia of cold therapy results from the reduced efficiency of pain receptors in cold conditions.

Easing of muscle spasm. As pain is reduced so muscle spasm begins to ease. Muscles go into spasm in reaction to pain — the tightness of this spasm further heightens the pain and interferes with the circulatory flow which, in turn, reduces the oxygen supply to the area. Any interference with the supply of oxygen may lead to degenerative changes and tissue death.

Hosing

The most common practice, hosing, should be carried out for approximately twenty minutes at least three times daily. The heels must be plugged with Vaseline and carefully dried after hosing to prevent cracking. It is possible to buy specially designed 'hose boots' which enable the horse to be left standing and save time spent holding the hosepipe. Great care is needed as the sole and frog quickly become soaked and the horn softens excessively. Iodine-based medications help prevent this. Some of the aquaboots compress the water jets, giving a jacuzzi-type massage. This reduces oedema and improves circulation.

Cold tubbing

A sturdy container may be filled with cold water and crushed ice. The horse then has to be encouraged to stand with the injured limb immersed for approximately fifteen minutes, two or three times a day. Precautions must again be taken to prevent cracked heels — pack heels with Vaseline and dry carefully afterwards.

Cold water bandages

In this traditional treatment, a bandage and gamgee are soaked in icy water and put into position. This dressing must be checked and replaced frequently, as the water soon warms up. Alternatively, pour ice water through the dressing regularly. Under no circumstances should the bandages be allowed to dry out on the limb because of the risk of shrinkage.

Because of the short amount of time it takes for the soaked gamgee to warm up, this cold treatment is not very effective.

Ice treatments

Because of the risk of ice burn, ice treatments must not be placed in direct contact with the skin. A layer of lint or similar should be placed between the ice pack and the skin. Prolonged exposure to intense cold may lead to ischaemia (tissue death as a result of reduced blood flow). Also, because of the vaso-constriction of the superficial blood vessels, ice treatments must not be in position for longer than thirty minutes on any one area. However, there are various types of specialist preparations available on the market. These include gel-filled sachets and bandages impregnated with gel which, once frozen, remain cold for up to three hours. These preparations are designed to reach a therapeutic temperature level, so may be used safely without the risk of tissue death.

More traditionally, gamgee may be soaked and frozen in the deep freeze. This can then be bandaged into position. The ice particles begin to melt once the dressing is in place. Another useful form of cold poultice is kaolin spread between two sheets of polythene and then frozen. This makes an economic, reusable cold dressing. It is a good idea to keep one or two ready frozen.

Heat therapy

Heat therapy should not be used if infection of the deeper tissues is suspected, since vasodilation can cause the spread of toxins. Nor should it be used in advance of other therapies (such as the administration of antibiotics) which may act to treat, and thus reduce, infection. However, the *localized* application of heat, as in poulticing and hot tubbing, can be useful in drawing out pus resulting from local, relatively mild, infection.

Short-wave diathermy

The deep tissues of the body (including bone) can be warmed by means of a machine emitting a high-frequency alternating current. Because damage can easily occur through overheating of the deep tissues, this machine must only be used by a qualified person. Furthermore, this treatment should never be carried out if bone screws or metalware are in place.

Poultices

Poultices help to relieve bruising, clean wounds, draw out infection and reduce inflammation.

To prevent burning, always ensure that poultices are not too hot when applied; test the temperature on the back of your hand. Common types of poultice are:

Animalintex, a ready prepared lint dressing which you simply cut to size and soak in very hot water. Wring out the excess water, apply to the injury and cover with polythene. Either bandage into position using gamgee as padding or, if using on an area where bandaging is impractical, hold in place with waterproof sticking plaster. Animalintex may also be used as a cold dressing.

Kaolin is a paste which is heated up in its tin — prise the lid loose and stand in a saucepan of boiling water. The paste may be spread on unbroken skin to reduce swelling, for example after a kick. Always test the temperature of kaolin carefully —

it can get very hot. When it is at the desired temperature, spread onto a piece of sterile cloth such as lint and stick directly onto the swelling, covering with gamgee held in position with sticking plaster.

Bran. If Animalintex is not available, hot bran makes a useful substitute when dealing with a wound of the foot. Make up a small bran mash adding 50 g (2 oz) of Epsom salts. The Epsom salts add to the drawing properties of the poultice. Place the bran in a stout polythene bag and place over the foot so that the injured area is covered with the wet, hot bran. Pad over with gamgee and bandage as previously described, using either a poultice boot or hessian sacking for additional protection.

Hot tubbing

This is a form of treatment to ease bruising of the lower leg, to draw out infection and clean puncture wounds. You will need a strong rubber bucket full of hand-hot water and Epsom salts. Place Vaseline in the heels, pick out and scrub the foot, then immerse the injured limb. The horse must be encouraged to stand still with his foot in the bucket. Add hot water regularly and keep the foot immersed for twenty minutes. Repeat at least twice daily.

Fomentation

Hot and cold fomentations can be used to help reduce swelling. To do this you need a bucket of very cold water, two small hand towels and a bucket of very hot water. Keep the kettle hot so that you can top up the hot water. Soak each towel and wring out the cold one. Hold this over the bruise for a minute or two, then wring out the very hot towel and hold that over the bruise. Repeating the alternate hot and cold will stimulate the circulation by causing the blood vessels to constrict then dilate. The blood and fluid which have gathered beneath the skin should start to disperse. You will need to do this for approximately twenty minutes at least three times a day until the bruising has eased.

Therapy machines

A wide range of specialist therapies is now available for the treatment of lameness. These therapies are in use by physiotherapists and other expert personnel at clinics and rehabilitation centres. Many of the machines are available to purchase, but it must be stressed that they should be used *in accordance with the vet's or physiotherapist's advice and only by a trained person.* Furthermore, the information which follows regarding the various machines and treatments should not be considered a substitute for the advice of an equine specialist. Advice must always be sought promptly for diagnostic and therapeutic purposes in the case of injury and/or lameness. Delay may lead to irreparable damage and permanent unsoundness.

Magnetic field therapy

Much research has gone into the effects of pulsating and static magnetic field therapy in the treatment of both hard (bone) and soft (muscle and tendon) tissue damage. Certain pulses of magnetic field improve circulation, which increases cell activity, so promoting the healing process. Research suggests that different pulses affect different tissues.

Pulsating magnetic field therapy may be administered through a mains operated machine or, if treating a leg injury, through a battery operated boot. Static magnetic field therapy is administered through the use of magnetic foil which remains in place almost continually.

The manufacturers give full treatment instructions which, with the advice of an expert, should be followed carefully.

Ultrasound

Sound may be defined as vibrating waves travelling through a medium such as air. The length, velocity and frequency of sound waves are measured in cycles per second which are expressed as hertz. A kilohertz (KHz) is 1000 cycles per second; a megahertz (MHz) is 1 million cycles per second. The normal range of human hearing is around 20 KHz. Ultrasound waves cannot be perceived by the human ear as they have a frequency well above this.

Ultrasonic waves are reflected by air; it causes the waves to bounce back upon themselves. However, they travel through liquid media and, when emitted from an ultrasound machine used by a trained person, ultrasonic waves may be used for scanning, measurement, diagnosis and treatment. When used as treatment, ultrasound waves are converted to heat in the tissues. The treatment is best used for deep heat penetration of muscles (to treat myositis) and for nerve damage, tendon injury, bursitis and scars. Blood flow is increased, helping to reduce inflammation and muscle spasm, and scar tissue may become more elastic after ultrasound treatment. It is not of value in cases of bone damage and can actually damage bone. For this reason, it should not be used over the spine. Furthermore, it should not be used in acute injuries (as it may cause haematoma formation) or over metal implants or recent surgical sites. Also, if used for too long, at too high a temperature, by an inexperienced person, damage may occur within the deep structures.

Ultrasound machines

The machines, originally designed for human usage, may have three frequency settings — 0.75 MHz, 1 MHz and 3 MHz. (Those used for diagnostic purposes have settings of 3.5, 5 or 7.5 MHz.) However, the most commonly used machines often have only the 1 MHz setting, which makes them less controllable when treating structures of differing depths.

The machines are mains operated, the generator being within an earthed metal box on which are the control dials. The dials control the setting of timing, intensity (ultrasonic waves are measured as watts/cm^2) and whether the waves are pulsed or continuous. Attached to the generator by a lead is the transducer, or treatment head. Attached to the metal plate of the transducer is a special type of crystal (usually quartz or barium titnate) which is capable of vibrating according to the setting of the machine (thus, at 1 MHz the crystal must vibrate at 1 million cycles per second). The high-frequency current is transmitted from the crystal to the metal plate, which produces an ultrasonic wave. This wave has to pass through a medium other than air — a special water-based coupling gel may be used or, in treating a limb, the affected area may be immersed in water.

The area to be treated is clipped closely. If the immersion method is being used, the affected limb is submerged in a strong tub of water. All air bubbles must be rubbed out of the hair so that the ultrasound waves are not reflected back. The treatment head is held parallel to the limb approximately 1−2 cm away and moved in a slow circular or parallel motion.

If the contact method is to be used, the treatment surface of the transducer and the area to be treated should be well covered in the coupling gel. The transducer is placed firmly onto the area to be treated and the machine timing and intensity set. As the beam travels through the coupling medium and the tissues of the body, its intensity is reduced. The effect of this is calculated and taken into account when treating the deeper structures. The lower the wattage per cm^2, the better. Damage may occur if the treatment sessions are continued for too long over a long period. With the contact method of treatment, the transducer head is moved in the same way as with the immersion method — it should be kept in motion to avoid overheating the tissue.

Laser

The word laser is an acronym: Light Amplification by Stimulated Emission of Radiation. Laser apparatus emits a beam of intense light which may be used for surgical, healing and/or analgesic purposes dependent upon the type of laser used.

High power or hot lasers actually destroy tissue through intense heat and have been used in various forms of surgery with success.

Low power or cold lasers do not destroy tissue, but have great therapeutic values. It is with these that we are chiefly concerned here.

When treatment is being given with a low power laser the laser beam may be emitted in a pulsed or continuous wave; a pulsed beam is effective for analgesic purposes, while a continuous beam is generally used for healing.

Laser has an analgesic effect when used correctly on the acupuncture points. This treatment must be carried out approximately once a week by a trained person familiar with the sites of the many acupuncture points.

If a continuous beam is used on an open wound, it penetrates the tissues and is absorbed by the cells, where it is acts as an extra energy source. This extra energy accelerates the healing process by helping collagen to be produced more rapidly. Also, because of the increased blood supply bringing white blood cells (leucocytes) to the site, bacterial contamination is reduced. (Further information on the role of leucocytes in combating infection can be found in another book in this series — *The Horse: Physiology*.)

Laser has been used to treat superficial joint and bone injuries, tendon and ligament conditions and old fibrous scar tissue. This treatment reduces the time taken to recover quite noticeably, even though there is no sensation felt by the horse while the beam is penetrating the damaged tissues.

Laser is generally effective to a depth of 10−15 mm, the depth of penetration and the effectiveness of the beam being dependent on the wavelength of the emitted beam frequency. This apparatus should only be used by a trained and skilled operator as, used wrongly, laser may have adverse effects on the injured site. Also, because of the risk of eye damage, it is important to wear *laser* goggles and to avoid looking directly at the laser source. There is much research still being carried out in the field of laser therapy.

Electrovet and Ionicare units

All cell membranes consist of electrically charged particles known as ions. After injury to any specific area the ionic balance of the tissue is disturbed, resulting in impaired transmission of nervous impulses and varying degrees of loss of function. The functions can only be restored fully when any ionic imbalance has been rectified. Once the nervous impulses are travelling in the normal manner, the muscles will receive stimulation — without stimulation muscle deteriorates, becoming atrophied.

There are two main types of machine devised to restore the correct ionic balance within the cells. These are the Electrovet and Ionicare systems. Both units consist of a surcingle containing a negative electrode. A pack mounted on the surcingle holds a small electrical generator which is run by rechargeable batteries. To be effective, the generator must be fully charged before use. The surcingle is buckled firmly into position over a folded towel and the control dial adjusted to either the 'leg' or 'muscle' setting.

The electrodes used to stimulate the injured area are covered in a special coupling gel and the area soaked with water. Electrodes on the leg may be held in position with bandages; those on the body may be hand-held. The leads from the machine to the electrodes are then connected, followed by the lead from the generator to the negative electrode on the surcingle. The machine operator will then slowly turn up the control dial until the horse indicates, by quivering or lifting the limb, that he can feel the current. The machine is then adjusted as appropriate and left for approximately two hours.

During this time the horse may stand tied up, with a haynet to keep him occupied. Once the equipment has been disconnected and removed, the treated area should be carefully washed and dried to avoid irritation of the skin.

Depending on which setting is chosen the machines are useful in the treatment of tendon and joint damage, bursal enlargements, muscle strain and atrophied muscle. According to the instructions of the vet or physiotherapist the treatment usually lasts for about three weeks.

Faradism

Faradism is the term often used to describe the artificial stimulation of muscle tissue with an electric current. Specialist training is essential as a deep knowledge of the muscles, their functions and their motor points is essential if faradism is to be of true benefit to the horse.

By means of a faradic machine the muscles may be stimulated with an electric (faradic) current, which causes the muscle fibres to contract. This helps to prevent muscle atrophy (wasting of the muscle through lack of stimulation) which may result from localized injury or interference with the nerve supply. Electrical stimulation improves venous and lymphatic movement, which results in improved circulation. As the muscle fibres are contracted so the strength may be developed, thus preventing further atrophy. Also, the movement of the muscle fibres helps to keep the formation of scar tissue and adhesions to a minimum. Another benefit is that the electrical stimulation improves venous and lymphatic movement, which results in improved circulation and reduced inflammation.

The easiest machine to use is the battery operated type which may be strapped around the operator's waist for ease of movement, the active electrode being hand-held. A faradic machine has two leads which have an electrode at one end. One is the active electrode and the other is termed indifferent. The electrodes and the area to be treated are soaked with a saline solution which acts as a good conductor of the electrical current. The electrodes generally consist of thin metal plates which must not come into direct contact with the skin — a thin layer of padding helps prevent irritation of the area. The area to be treated may be covered in coupling gel so that the active electrode can glide over the hair when moved from one motor point to another. A motor point is the place at which a motor nerve enters a muscle and branches off into a network of smaller nerves. It is at these points that stimulation should be directed to achieve maximum muscle contraction.

The indifferent electrode is strapped onto an area just behind the withers by means of a roller and pad. The most comfortable sensation is felt by the horse if the roller is firmly done up. The operator has the machine fastened around the waist with all controls switched off. The lead from the indifferent pad is attached to the machine. The lead from the hand-held active pad is then also attached to the machine and positioned on the relevant motor nerve. The trained operator will judge the necessary speed of the muscle contraction required (the surge) and the intensity of the electrical stimulus, and adjust the dials accordingly. The muscle is then stimulated some twenty to thirty times before moving on to the next muscle. The muscle must not be overstimulated — fatigue may occur if is not allowed to rest.

Electrical stimulation of muscle may also be used for diagnostic purposes. This is achieved by comparing the reactions of healthy and the corresponding unhealthy muscles. The horse may show signs of pain when a damaged muscle is stimulated. Also, weakened or damaged muscles will require a stronger stimulus — the intensity of the necessary current is recorded and comparisons made throughout the course of treatment.

Massage

Used in conjunction with other forms of treatment to reduce inflammation, massage can have highly therapeutic qualities. It improves the local circulation, resulting in an increase in the rate at which waste products are removed from the area. There are two main types of massage:

Friction massage. When massaging the limbs, in particular the tendons, most benefit is gained from small movements concentrated in one area — the fingers press, following the line of the tissues beneath the skin. A lubricant should be used to allow the fingers to slide easily over the coat.

Mechanical massage machines. These may be hand-held units or specialized adhesive pads. The affected area of the limb should be fitted with a tube-grip stocking and the machine worked over this to prevent a skin reaction. The horse should initially be allowed to become used to a low level of vibration, which can gradually be increased. Treatment will probably be necessary three times daily, for thirty minutes per session, continued until the condition has noticeably improved.

Support

Support is an important aid in preventing excessive inflammation of an area. After cold treatments have been administered, support bandages should be used to prevent a sudden surge of blood and fluids back to the area.

When bandaging for support, a wide elasticated bandage should be used over a decent amount of padding. The bandage should extend from just below the knee or hock to the coronet. Do not bandage in the same way as when applying support bandages for exercise, as the area left unbandaged between the fetlock and coronet will fill with fluid very quickly.

Pressure bandages must be removed regularly and the legs massaged to encourage healthy circulation before the bandages are replaced. The contralateral limb must always be bandaged as it will be subjected to extra strain.

Anti-inflammatory drugs

When an area becomes damaged, a chemical known as arachidonic acid is released. This is then acted upon by an enzyme called cyclo-oxygenase. The result of this interaction is the conversion of arachidonic acid into prostaglandins, the chemicals which cause the symptoms of heat, pain and swelling as well as increasing the sensitivity of pain receptors in the area.

Anti-inflammatory drugs which may be administered to reduce the painful effects of inflammation can be divided into two groups:

Corticosteroids. Cortisol, a natural compound, was used originally in anti-inflammatory corticosteroids but it is now more common for synthetic corticosteroids to be used. The exact manner in which these drugs act on inflammation is not definitely known, but it is considered that they act within the nuclei of the affected cells, causing an alteration to the production of proteins. Their anti-inflammatory effects are described more fully in another book in the series — *The Horse: The Foot, Shoeing and Lameness.* Corticosteroids may be injected directly into the inflamed area (for example, into a joint) or administered intravenously. Generally, a single dose can be given without serious side effects, but prolonged treatment can be dangerous. Also, since they inhibit the healing process and suppress the immune response, they should not be used in open wounds or in the presence of infection.

Non-steroidal anti-inflammatory drugs. These drugs are chemically unrelated to cortisol, being of a different chemical structure. The non-steroidal drugs in use include the well known phenyl-butazone (bute) and less well known meclofenamic acid, flunixin, meglamine and naproxen. These drugs act by neutralizing the enzyme cyclo-oxygenase — without this chemical catalyst the arachidonic acid cannot be converted into prostaglandins, so the signs of inflammation will subside.

All drugs should be administered under veterinary advice as all produce side effects and the random use of them, particularly if given in too large a dosage, can have serious long-term effects. Furthermore, if it is necessary to administer drugs to a horse who is due to compete, the 'Forbidden Substances' section of the relevant rule book must be consulted. (Obviously, in such cases, the horse's long-term welfare must take precedence over his eligibility for a particular competition.)

The subject of drugs and their effect on the horse is discussed more fully in another book in this series, *The Horse: Physiology*.

Blistering and firing

These so-called 'therapies' have become less common, indeed firing is now illegal in the UK.

Blisters involve the application of an irritant substance such as mercuric iodide which causes inflammation and blistering. The idea behind them is that circulation will be improved to bring about healing, thus benefiting the damaged tendons, and that the resultant scar tissue will provide a strengthened support to the area.

Firing was supposed to produce the same results — the skin being pierced either in parallel lines (line firing), or in a matrix of dots (pin firing), by a red-hot iron. Research proved that firing did not enhance the healing process, in fact it hindered it and caused unnecessary suffering to the horse.

Although firing is illegal, some still advocate the use of blisters and it is the responsibility of the horse owner to decide whether or not to subject the horse to further discomfort, particularly when so many effective, non-irritant, analgesic therapies are available.

RECOVERY AND REHABILITATION

After any injury there will be the need for a period of recovery and rehabilitation, the duration and nature of which will depend upon the severity of the condition. Post-operative recovery is obviously a specialist subject requiring the expertise of the veterinary team and the clinic facilities.

The object of rehabilitation is to restore to normality the injured tissue and/or bone through repair and re-education (encouraging the restored tissue and attendant structures to function correctly). The repair process may be aided by physiotherapy — the selective use of machines will promote healing and reduce pain.

Traditionally, the majority of horses are turned away to rest immediately after the injury has occurred — if the injury is causing discomfort it will lead to the horse moving in an unbalanced way to compensate. This movement may well become established, developing an uneven gait and muscular build-up which will probably be maintained upon full recovery. As the horse is constantly moving out of balance the old injury is likely to recur or indeed, a new injury may result. Correct rehabilitation before the horse is turned away to rest can greatly improve the chances of a full and balanced recovery, resulting in prolonged soundness and a successful return to his competitive career.

Therefore, during treatment and rehabilitation the physiotherapist, vet and owner will need to work closely together, monitoring the horse's reaction to treatment and his progress. When the vet and physiotherapist are in agreement, re-education can commence.

Swimming, which may be included in the rehabilitation programme, is very useful as the horse's limbs bear no weight. However, care must be taken to ensure that each limb is used evenly to promote even muscular development. The heart-rate monitor should be used as the horse may become easily stressed if unused to swimming. Walking in water, particularly against a current, is also very beneficial. The sea is ideal, otherwise a safe stream or wading area at a pool can be used.

Straight line work at the walk on long-reins can, if carried out properly, help to even out muscular imbalances. Circle work would exert too much strain on the muscles and joints.

Once a high level of recovery has been achieved, basic ridden schooling can supple and strengthen muscles as well as helping to improve balance. Steady work over raised poles improves rhythm and tempo whilst encouraging the horse to flex his joints effectively. When at the riding stage of the rehabilitation programme, it is important to appreciate that correct shoeing, bitting, care of teeth and saddle fitting will all affect the horse's chances of staying in balance.

CONCLUSION

The title 'Competition Horse' encompasses every equine ranging from those competing at a local riding club event to those at an international three day event.

The higher one goes up the competition ladder, the greater the emphasis which must be placed on a thorough and appropriate fittening and training programme. Nevertheless, the basic principles of fittening apply to *all* horses. It can be both harmful and dangerous to compete on a horse who is not suitably prepared. Possible results may include falls, damage to the respiratory system, heart or limbs and/or exhaustion. Competing in hot and/or humid conditions brings the additional risks of dehydration and heatstroke.

The best way to learn how to fitten a horse is to follow expert advice and then actually do it – set your goal and plan your programme but never forget that horses are all individuals; what suits one may not suit another. Also, be prepared to adjust your programme if soundness problems (of either horse or rider) or adverse weather conditions intervene.

Above all, do not ignore or skip over the following essentials:

Plan a workable programme suitable to your goals.

Allow ample time for the basic fittening work.

161

Most importantly . . . treat each horse as an individual and adapt your programme as necessary.

Whatever the type and level of competition, the fundamental requirement is to have a well prepared, fit and sound horse upon which to compete. Then you, the rider, can concentrate upon making the most of it . . . Good luck!

BIBLIOGRAPHY

Bullock, J. *Transporting Horses by Road*. Threshold Books Ltd., 1986.

Clarke, A.F. and Jeffcott, L.B. *On to Atlanta '96*. The Equine Research Centre, Ontario, Canada, 1994.

Leng, V. *Training the Event Horse*. Stanley Paul & Co. Ltd., 1990.

Pilliner, S. *Getting Horses Fit*. Collins, 1986.

Snow, Dr. D.H. and Vogel, C.J. *Equine Fitness — The Care and Training of the Athletic Horse*. David and Charles, 1987.

Todd, M. *Mark Todd's Cross Country Handbook*. The Kenilworth Press Ltd., 1991.

INDEX

165